WRITING WITH EMOTION, TENSION, & CONFLICT

CHERYL ST. JOHN

For more resources for writers, visit www.writersdigest.com.

20 19 18 17   12 11 10 9 8 7

Distributed in Canada by Fraser Direct
100 Armstrong Avenue
Georgetown, Ontario, Canada L7G 5S4
Tel: (905) 877-4411

Distributed in the U.K. and Europe by F+W Media International
Brunel House, Newton Abbot, Devon, TQ12 4PU, England
Tel: (+44) 1626-323200, Fax: (+44) 1626-323319
E-mail: postmaster@davidandcharles.co.uk

Distributed in Australia by Capricorn Link
P.O. Box 704, Windsor, NSW 2756 Australia
Tel: (02) 4577-3555

Edited by Rachel Randall
Designed by Terri Woesner
Cover designed by Claudean Wheeler
Production coordinated by Debbie Thomas

media

 DEDICATION

To authors everywhere who work tirelessly to create the best stories possible, who push themselves to improve their craft, and who bring hours of pleasure to others through the written word, and to aspiring authors who are reading these concepts for the first time and wondering how they will ever be able to do all this. We've all been there. You can do it, too.

ACKNOWLEDGMENTS

I've had a lot of help and encouragement along my writing journey. The late Diane Wicker Davis read my first attempt at a manuscript and offered gentle guidance. Barbara Andrews invited me to a group at her home and was one of the first to tell me I had what it took to write a good story. Pam Hart started a critique group and tirelessly read my pages and offered suggestions. My education on the craft of writing began with these generous and gifted women.

Techniques of the Selling Writer by Dwight V. Swain made the most impact as far as comprehending the elements of storytelling and learning skills to engage readers. I devoured every Nancy Kress article I ever found and studied my favorite authors. Once I sold, my editor Margaret O'Neil Marbury showed me how to effectively break the rules I'd so earnestly learned and followed.

I'm thankful to every person who ever attended one of my workshops or took one of my online classes and gave me feedback. I appreciate all the authors quoted in this book and those whose excerpts I used to show examples of great storytelling. Thank you to my critique group for their proofreading, brilliant suggestions, and continued support, career-wise and personally. Thank you to my agent Pam Hopkins for always being in my corner, to F+W Media for taking on this book, and to Rachel Randall for acquiring and editing my first nonfiction project.

ABOUT THE AUTHOR

Cheryl is the author of more than fifty books. Her first book, *Rain Shadow,* was nominated for Romance Writers of America's RITA Award for Best First Book, by *Romantic Times Magazine* for Best Western Historical, and by *Affaire de Coeur* readers for Best American Historical Romance. Since then she has received three more RITA nominations, a *Writer's Digest* award for a feature article, and several Romantic Times Reviewers Choice awards. Many of her books were featured in Waldenbooks Top Ten lists and *USA Today*, and *Big Sky Brides* climbed to #35 on the NYT list.

Cheryl has been a keynote speaker numerous times and has taught workshops at Romance Writers of America National Conference, American Christian Fiction Writers National Conference, Romantic Times Booklovers Convention, Mid-America RWA Conference, Desert Dreams Conference, Orange County RWA, Midwest Mystery and Suspense Convention, University of Nebraska at Omaha Writers Conference, Nebraska Literature Festival, Nebraska Writers Guild, Rocky Mountain Book Festival, Friends of the Public Library, Romance Authors of the Heartland, Iowa Romance Novelists, Prairie Romance Writers, and Carolina Romance Writers.

Cheryl has had articles on the craft of writing published in Romance Writers of America's *Romance Writers Report* and in numerous chapter newsletters. She was featured in the *Writer's Digest Romance Writer's Sourcebook,* and the UK magazine *Writer's Forum* featured her in a two-page article. Cheryl's online workshops have garnered praise from new writers and multipublished authors alike.

In describing her stories of second chances and redemption, readers and reviewers use words like "emotional punch, hometown feel, core values, believable characters, and real-life situations." Amazon and Goodreads reviews show her popularity with readers.

One thing all reviewers and readers agree on regarding Cheryl's work is the degree of emotion and believability. Words like "heartwarming, emotional depth, endearing characters" and "on my keeper shelf" are commonly used to describe her work.

TABLE OF CONTENTS

INTRODUCTION

Like most of you who have opened this book, I read voraciously as a young person. I vividly remember how disappointed I was over summer breaks because my access to the school library was suspended. I still recall my favorite stories, the characters, and the feelings they created. Books were my companions. They spoke to me. They incited dreams and sparked my imagination.

I'm often asked when I began writing, and the fact is I can't remember a time when I didn't write. As a child I wrote stories, drew covers, and stapled them into little books. My first rejection came at the tender age of fourteen, when I sent a story to *Redbook* magazine. I still have that half-page rejection slip. I learned early that not every story hits its mark. Eventually I understood why: Some manuscripts deserve to be in a drawer.

What I didn't learn for a long time—years, actually—was that there are techniques proven to help create stories with depth and broad appeal. Techniques that bring a story from the writer's head onto the printed page in a form appealing to both readers and publishers. Techniques that make the reader feel strongly about your story.

Probably the most important concept I've taken away from any book on writing is from Dwight V. Swain's *Techniques of the Selling Writer*: A story is *feelings*. In order for a reader to connect with a story, he must feel that he has a stake in the character's plight and must care about the outcome. If you can create an emotional connection, you can hold your reader's attention. You can prompt him to read on and even to buy your next book.

If you want to forge an emotional connection with your reader, you must first master the skills involved. Understand that you're not guaranteed success. There is no magic involved, and no secret formula exists. Multipublished authors aren't holding out on you. Most successful people worked a long time to achieve their goals. Success is not easy or instant. Some writers do sell their first book, but the percentage is small. Forget the get-rich-quick scheme, and look the task ahead squarely in the eye. Acknowledge the complexity of fiction, and accept the time and effort required to make your work marketable. Successful people know how to delay gratification.

❝❞

You might have more talent than me, you might be smarter than me, but you will never outwork me.
—WILL SMITH

Reading published books is necessary, but reading alone isn't enough. Reading a masterfully written book might make writing look easy, but just because you've got a Thomas Kinkade painting on your wall doesn't make you qualified to paint one.

There are writers who will tell you they refuse to write to a formula and, therefore, don't appreciate instruction or constructive criticism. Is technique a formula? In a sense, yes. Every movie you've ever watched was developed from a screenplay—a formula. But there are so many combinations of ways to put words together, use setting, and develop characters that the finished products are not formulaic.

When I read those books that shaped my love of writing, when I discovered authors whose words spoke to me on an emotional level, I knew then I wanted to write stories that would affect people the same way. Over the years I dabbled with short stories and wrote longhand in notebooks. Eventually I toyed with longer stories.

I had written several book-length manuscripts by the time I took on a larger project than I'd ever before attempted. It was the year my youngest child went to school, and I made up my mind that this would be the time I got serious and wrote a real book. I spent hours researching at the library, and I cluelessly used every bit of my research. And then I edited. And edited. And edited. I was in love with that story.

I'd seen an article in the Sunday paper about a national writers' group forming a local chapter. I was too cowardly to go. I wasn't a real writer. The writer featured in the article was a criminal justice teacher. I was a mom with a writing hobby. I'd read all the outdated how-to books from my library and I had a current copy of *Writer's Market*, so I began submitting on my own.

A pile of rejection letters followed.

The local chapter made my newspaper again. My brother, bless his heart, brought it to me on Easter and said, "You've got to get with these people. You're working in a vacuum." Eventually I garnered my courage and attended that writers' group, where I met people just like me, from all walks of life, who shared the same love of books and writing. And one fateful day an author I respected offered to read my manuscript. With fear and trembling I gave her three chapters. And then I waited.

At the next meeting she took me aside and kindly showed me her edits. Page after page had been X-ed through, and in the margins she'd written in red pen, "Nothing happening." It took me weeks to recover. But when I did, and when I studied her remarks and the changes she'd made, I saw exactly what she was talking about. How do you master all the various techniques and learn what works and what doesn't? By writing stories. A lot of them. By being willing to be wrong. By dancing naked on the table.

Swain says in *Techniques of the Selling Writer*, "Then having been wrong, you check back through your stuff for process errors, places where you skipped over steps or went off the path, or started with the roadmap upside down. Do that enough times, on enough stories, and eventually you'll learn."

Now some writers would have spent all their time and energy on that same book, still editing and still revising, but I set it aside. And I set out to write a different book—smartest thing I ever did—applying all the things I'd learned. An agent told me she could sell that next book, and she did. And then I asked the editor who bought it if she'd take a look at that first one. She did, and she told me if I cut a hundred pages (mostly the research), she'd buy it.

I had seven years of study and bad writing under my belt before I knew enough to write to sell. And even then—even now—I still have projects that don't work.

I can tell you the book and the moment that changed everything for me. The idea for my fourth book, *Saint or Sinner*, came from an old movie starring Joanne Woodward as a young girl and Van Heflin as a man with a shady past. It wasn't the plot or Woodward's character that fascinated me; it was the character who came back from war a changed man. Life is all about second chances, and it's a theme that resonates with all of us. We've all needed a do-over more than once. So I created a man fresh from the war, bent on starting over.

The heroine for this story is as prim and uptight as a person can be—rigid, unyielding—with others and with herself. Because she has a secret, a past filled with abuse and shame, she attempts to rise above it by becoming someone she's not. As most of us know, this rarely works. We have to own who we are and what has happened in our pasts and rise above it. So it's a story of redemption and personal victories.

I lived a short distance from a small local post office, where I kept my post-office box for fan mail. In those days, people actually wrote letters, not e-mails, so once a week I'd drive to the post office. I often sat in my car in front of the building and opened the envelopes with a letter opener I kept handy just for that purpose. That day I read a letter from a young woman for whom my story rang not only true but personal. She told me how her stepfather had beaten her until she had suffered permanent nerve damage in her arm. She said she was alone but that my story had given her hope that one day she would know someone who loved her as much as Joshua loved Addie. I don't know how I managed to drive home through my tears.

I sat at my desk with tears running down my face, hurting for this girl I'd never met. In those moments everything I did seemed trivial. Pointless. I sat in my comfortable, air-conditioned office with everything I needed at my fingertips, sipping tea, and just *making up* these stories. I created fiction, but she had lived a tragedy. I felt small and petty.

But then, within minutes, I realized I had at last made the magical connection. The ideas and characters that had taken shape in my head had traveled to the page, through the editing and publication process, off the press, and into the store—straight into that reader's hands and into her heart and mind. The story I created had given her hope. Hope, redemption, forgiveness, and love are things we all want and need.

That connection is what every writer wants. We need to share our stories in such a way that they resonate with readers. I believe the craft of writing is learnable. The stories are there for the telling, but the techniques are more elusive. Those first attempts aren't satisfying—in fact, they're downright frustrating—because the words don't come out the way we want them to, the way we imagine. The people and the scenes are in our heads, scrolling like a movie, unveiling like a conversation or a narration, but what makes it to the page is a poor substitute for our imagination. The good news is that writing improves with practice. Voice is developed over pages and pages and pages—thousands of them.

There are a lot of books and articles on writing. Always look at the source. Study the instructor's work. Don't write by anyone else's rules without knowing that the concept behind a rule works and is proven to work. Find out why the rule came into being. Rules you don't understand are restrictive. Knowing why rules exist sets you free to follow or break them with wisdom and expertise. You have to learn the rules to know when to break them to your advantage and to the story's advantage.

Feeling tells you what to say. Technique gives you the tools with which to say it.

I've created this book as a study guide with exercises meant to be completed. I don't claim to have all the answers. I still learn something every day. The answers I do have must be discovered in your own time and by your own process, but I've developed these chapters and exercises to provoke those discoveries. You will benefit most from the study if you dedicate a notebook or journal right now, make your own lists, and note your discoveries as you read.

I believe if you have the gift of storytelling and the desire to learn, you can write a book worthy of submission. This book is for you, dear writer.

HOW TO GET THE MOST FROM THIS BOOK

You will get the most from this book if you start a binder, notebook, or journal right now, Today. Most of us retain information by taking notes, so make lists and take notes on the key elements you want to remember. Use divider tabs for each section. Do the exercises.

I'm not a believer in doing exercises just for the sake of getting words on pages, though I know many are, so do whatever works for you. Personally, I want every written word to move a project forward, so all the exercises within these chapters are geared specifically toward your book. You should be able to take your completed pages and use them as notes for your book, as part of your synopsis, or as actual pages and paragraphs for your story.

Treat your notebook with importance. Take the exercises seriously. We learn by doing. We learn by discovering things on our own. I can explain conflict to you, but until you dissect it yourself and understand the internal workings, you won't have grasped how to set it up in your own stories.

Whenever I mention a movie, you will benefit by watching it—even if you've seen it before. I try to take my examples from familiar movies. I have watched certain movies numerous times for study. I always learn something about the plotting or characters or about myself and my reactions. Netflix or Amazon Prime streaming are awesome tools for an afternoon of study. Remember that movie watching is work and you're learning something during the process, even if your study includes popcorn. Use your journal or binder when you watch movies. Take notes. You'll be a better writer for it.

Movies for your Netflix queue:

- *You've Got Mail*
- *Jaws*
- *Jerry Maguire*
- *Face/Off*
- *Pay It Forward*
- *Die Hard*
- *Practical Magic*
- *Runaway Bride*
- *The Rock*
- *Erin Brockovich*
- *Slumdog Millionaire*
- *While You Were Sleeping*
- *Bridesmaids*
- *Rain Man*

Recommended reading:

- *Techniques of the Selling Writer*, Dwight V. Swain, University of Oklahoma Press, 1982
- *GMC: Goal, Motivation & Conflict*, Debra Dixon, Gryphon Books for Writers, 1999
- *Writing on Both Sides of the Brain*, Henriette Anne Klauser, Harper & Row, 1986

PART ONE
CONFLICT MAKES THE STORY

[1]
DEFINING
CONFLICT

Movies to watch: *Jaws, You've Got Mail*

I preface every workshop, every critique, and each answer to a writing question with this statement: I will never tell you there is only one way to approach a story or that one technique for writing is the only correct technique.

What I can and will assure you is this: The right way—the most effective way to do anything—is the way that works for you. So while I have learned much on my writing journey, I can only teach you to observe, analyze, and study the effective techniques and offer you tools to test for yourself.

I became a student of Dwight V. Swain's *Techniques of the Selling Writer* in my early writing days. To this day writers get a glazed look in their eyes when this book is mentioned. A writer I trust recommended it to me, and I remember attempting to read it at my regular reading time for several weeks. Unfortunately, I often schedule my reading time just before bedtime, so the book put me to sleep more nights than I want to admit. I was determined, however, so I made time during the day to study Swain's advice. It was a momentous occasion when the light bulb came on and I actually understood how to apply the advice to my work. I got it. I actually got it! And I could see how his techniques applied to every great story I'd ever read and how I could apply them to my own work. I studied all the books on my "favorites" shelf and discovered that, yes, his techniques were there and had been all along, but they were so beautifully executed that it took an educated eye to see them.

I never miss an opportunity to encourage a writer to study Swain's book, so if you don't own a copy, I suggest you purchase one and add it to your must-study reads. No one explains the concept of scene/sequel better. Debra Dixon has condensed Swain's goal, motivation, and conflict chapters into her own book, which I like to call the "Swain Cliffs Notes," actually titled *GMC: Goal, Motivation & Conflict*. Grab a copy of that one, too, if you don't have one. No, really, I insist. Instruction books are an investment in your craft and career. And they're tax deductible.

I've given online workshops, conference workshops, and local classes on the topic of conflict for years. I found it eye-opening to discover how many writers have taken the class a second time. I was also interested by how many students were already multipublished. This told me that plotting conflict is a skill all of us can stand to improve and must stay focused on. A true sign of maturity is a writer who can look at his or her own work objectively and who has a desire to grow and stretch. My objective in these first chapters is to challenge your thinking, to encourage you to be the best you can be, and to give you insight on how to develop your stories with built-in conflict.

Conflict isn't something you can tack on later, once you've written half the book and realize it's going nowhere. It's not something you can generate as you write. Just throwing things at your character to see what will stick only makes for an episodic[1] series of events. One

---

[1] *Episodic* means that scenes don't relate to each other and have been strung together without purpose. I knew a writer who made lists of things she thought would be great to write, wrote the scenes, and then tried to connect them. The stories she came up with were disconnected and rambling because the scenes weren't tied together. Every action has a reaction, so each scene must spring from the previous one.

of the most familiar reasons editors give for declining a manuscript is that there is "not enough conflict to sustain a story." Ouch. I received plenty of those rejections when I was a beginner. In future chapters I'll talk to you about internal and external conflict. External conflicts are circumstances and other characters. Not every story has to have a personified villain. You will see I use movies as examples and comparisons because they're universal and more people are likely to have seen a particular one than to have read the same book. I treated myself to seeing *The Help* the week it was released. In *The Help*, there are villain-like characters, but the true antagonist is discrimination and racial prejudice. This external conflict feeds into the characters' internal conflicts. Each protagonist has a clear goal and believable motivation, and each must make difficult decisions to overcome her conflicts. It is definitely worth seeing and taking notes. A few other successful plots that rely heavily on external conflict are *Avatar*, *Face/Off*, and *Jurassic Park*. I'm sure there are a million more.

In order to understand conflict and how to develop it, we must first understand what conflict is and what it's not. The elements that make up a story are so closely enmeshed that at times it becomes difficult to dissect and make a firm delineation between them. In a masterfully developed story, characterization, plotting, and conflict are all intricately entwined.

SO, WHAT IS CONFLICT?

Conflict is anything that hinders your character's effort to get what she wants. Conflict is another person or a group of people stopping your character from reaching her goal. It might also be an inhibiting and possibly fatal situation, like terrifying weather or an asteroid hurtling toward Earth.

Webster's Dictionary defines conflict as "the opposition of persons or forces that gives rise to the dramatic action in a drama or fiction." This definition is the essence of fiction, and we need to keep it in mind as we develop characters and plots.

If there's no conflict, there's no story.

In order for conflict to exist, each character must have a concrete goal. Otherwise, conflict is only a nuisance. The made-for-TV movie *Meteor* contains a whole lot of delay and external conflict. The main characters' goal was to stop the destruction of the world. The old scientist (played by Christopher Lloyd, who had the all-important coordinates) and his young female assistant set off to take their information to the powers that be. The old scientist is hit by a car and killed right off the bat—big conflict for his assistant, who grabs the laptop and attempts to make the journey on her own. Holy cow, does that chick meet up with bad situations! In Mexico, prisoners pretending to be police attack her, and she manages to escape them. After locating real police officers while trying to get through a blockade, she gets thrown in jail for possessing a gun she took from the bad guys. She faces one trial after another. I'm reminded of Dorothy in *The Wizard of Oz*. Her goal was to get home to Auntie Em, and one situation after another kept her from getting there.

You will notice that in an adventure movie, we are always shown a main core of viewpoint characters. We're introduced to their daily lives, family situations, or jobs. This is what makes us care about whether or not the asteroid hits or if they contract the Super Flu. In order for the conflict to matter, we have to care.

Conflict is relative.

Conflict is brought to life by the character's motivation and reactions. What constitutes conflict for one person may be taken in stride or even considered an ideal situation for the next person. If you were a writer with a bad knee, and you required surgery and had to stay off your leg for a couple of weeks, of course you would be inconvenienced. Someone would have to shop for your groceries and walk the dog, but on the upside, you'd get in a lot of movie watching and plotting time. However, if you were a mail carrier requiring the same surgery, the time off your feet would present an entirely different dilemma because your livelihood would be at stake.

In order to have conflict, your character must have a goal and his goal must be believable. The believability factor comes from motivation. Your character must want something that fits in one of these three categories:

* Possession of something
* Relief from something
* Revenge for something

The goal must be specific and concrete—simple enough to state in one sentence. In my book *Marrying the Preacher's Daughter*, the heroine, Elizabeth, wants a man just like her father. Why is it believable? Because her father is a man she admires.

Without that goal, there would be no conflict when a man completely unlike her father rescues her and is shot, forcing her to take care of him. We have to make it difficult for our characters to reach their goals. It's our job to throw opposition at them and keep telling them *no*. Get your mean face on.

When we first start writing, many of us have difficulty giving our characters sufficient conflict. It's our nature to love them, nurture them, fix things for them—it's rather like they're our beloved children. But we can't fix these story people if they aren't broken. They can't grow if they don't have room to improve. It's your job to unfold the plot in such a way that your story people are forced to earn their happy ending. In order for the reader to root for them, your protagonists must deserve their happily ever afters.

Conflict will be different for each character, depending on how you create him. A great example of relative conflict is in a movie we all know: *Jaws*. The three main characters are Police Chief Martin Brody, Matt Hooper, and Quint. In analyzing the main characters' motivations, it becomes clear that each character has a different goal.

Chief Brody is a family man and the sheriff/chief of police. It's his job to protect the community. He is responsible, and he takes his responsibility seriously. When the body of the swimmer, Chrissie, is found, he goes on alert and wants to close the beach. His conflict at that point is that the mayor refuses to close the beach because summer income is the town's livelihood and the 50th annual regatta is about to take place.

So the shark eats the boy, Alex. Blaming Brody, the boy's mother seeks him out in public and slaps him. Brody is responsible for the boy's death because he didn't close the beach. Stopping the shark is now *personal*. He feels guilty for Alex's death, and he must keep the rest of the people safe. For the remainder of the movie, his conflict is, of course, the larger-than-life antagonist who keeps eating people. Brody is scared spitless, but because of his conviction, *we care* and are behind him 100 percent.

Matt Hooper is an oceanographer and young scientist. He shows up for the purpose of scientific research. When he finds Ben Gardner dead and sees the great white shark tooth, his goal becomes a gleeful mission. He has a backstory: When he was twelve, a shark ate his boat. Sharks have been his life's work ever since. He was on his way to Spain to study great whites for eighteen months, but now that there is one right here, he's eager to stay and find it. For Hooper, it's all about the thrill of the hunt and the scientific discovery. He's having the time of his life on this shark hunt.

Salty local fisherman Quint pops up at the town meeting and confidently offers to catch the shark for the hefty sum of ten thousand dollars or two hundred dollars a day, whether he gets the shark or not. His is a mercenary goal—or so it seems. His character is stereotypical with his limericks and sea songs and tales of the sea, but then he shares an insightful experience about being on the ship that delivered the bomb to Hiroshima. He tells of his ship sinking and watching his shipmates being eaten by sharks. Ah hah—backstory and motivation. Now we wonder if maybe his goal is more vengeful than mercenary, especially when he snaps, breaks the radio, and burns out the engine, marooning them in the sea with the killer shark. Now there's no way they can turn back.

This is an important lesson to remember: It's effective to eliminate all possibility that the character could go back to life as usual. He can no longer return to an ordinary world.

Every step of the way, the reader must know why this particular situation is important and why he should care. As you saw with *Jaws*, each character's situation was important to him, and we cared *because* of his motivation.

None of the three main characters in *Jaws* could have walked away from the hunt for the shark. They were in it to win it because they were motivated. We were on the edges of our seats and rooting for them because of the conflict—and because we cared about what happened to them. Conflict is danger to the goal. And danger is relative.

I use extreme examples because they illuminate the techniques so vividly. Not every story has a shark or a murderer or a life-and-death situation. This is where the *relative* part comes in.

Conflict is intolerable.

Conflict must be an intolerable state of affairs; it must be derived from problems or situations that your characters cannot ignore or explain away.

Your character should *do* something to remedy his situation. Chief Brody argued with the mayor's poor decisions, kept a vigil to protect the townspeople, and eventually went in search of the shark himself. As scared as he was, in the end he was the one to kill the shark.

Conflict is not delay.

Now and then we use incidents to show frustration, to characterize, or to flesh out the story and make the situation realistic. But even though these incidents are useful, they don't complicate the situation or make it worse; therefore, they are not truly conflict.

Examples of incidents:

* The protagonist can't find someone or something.
* She falls in a mud puddle.
* She loses her keys.
* She misses a bus.
* She arrives late at an important event.

Ever notice how the key never works in the car ignition the first time an axe murderer or a zombie bashes against the car windows? Then the rattled woman drops the key ring on the floor of the car and has to grope for it. This is only delay. It is effective to a point, but the true conflict is that crazed guy with the axe.

Conflict is not anger, bickering, or foot stomping.

This is probably one of the most widely misunderstood elements and one I see repeatedly in the stories of beginning writers. Beginning romance writers often write page after page of characters arguing and getting ticked off at each other. Getting mad and yelling at another character without reasonable, *believable* motivation only makes that character childish or just plain mean. This type of behavior is acceptable for antagonists because it characterizes them, but your protagonists must have more depth.

If you have a scene or two of bickering in your story, take a harsh look at it. Have another reader take a look at it and give his honest opinion. Is the argument motivated? Are there deeply held beliefs and principles behind the words? Are the feelings behind the words *emotional*?

You might be thinking of a story or a movie in which this kind of bickering works. There are always exceptions to the rule. *The African Queen* and *High Road to China* are movies in which the characters argue relentlessly, but for these particular story people and situations, the verbal sparring works because it's believable. The key is to make your characters' personalities work for your story.

Conflict is not the characters fighting with each other. It's them fighting with themselves.

A disagreement that can be cleared up with a brief explanation or a civil discussion between the main characters is not conflict. It's merely a misunderstanding.

Misunderstandings are fine and many of the novels we read start out that way, but misinterpretations between adults are easily discussed and cleared up. A story must have conflict beyond the initial misunderstanding, or that misunderstanding must be the catalyst for something more significant.

Often, when a person is angry, he's angry with himself or with an unresolved situation. Dig deeper.

Changes are difficult to make. We know we should behave one way, but our instinct is to behave just the opposite. This is three-dimensional characterizing. Having a character think one thing or want one thing but do the opposite is interesting—and it's his own personal conflict.

The more you build the conflict into your character, the easier the story is to write. No matter what writing topic I teach, I hang the most importance on characters. The most effective conflict is drawn directly from your story people. The conflict should be based on your characters' goals, backstories, and motivations. It should represent opposing forces that come from within the characters themselves.

Here's a classic example of conflict in *You've Got Mail*. Kathleen Kelly, owner of a small bookstore for children's books, secretly and anonymously e-mails a man she met in a chat room. She asks and accepts advice from her anonymous mail-pal. The opening of Fox Books discount store endangers her business. She meets Joe Fox, son of the owner, and is annoyed by his arrogant way of managing business. Eventually she has to close her store. Joe Fox learns that his e-mail friend is Kathleen Kelly, but he doesn't let on.

In *You've Got Mail*, the conflict is built into the characters before they ever meet, because they have opposing goals and both want the same market share of the book business. For Kathleen, it's personal—the store was once her mother's, and therefore the danger of losing it is emotional.

Feelings must be part of every effective conflict. Why? *Because a story is feelings.*

Not all conflict has to be life threatening or earth shattering. The world and all civilization won't come to an end if Kathleen loses her store, but it *is* important to her. Just for the record, I don't like the movie's resolution, and I think Tom Hanks's character is still a jerk at the end. She ends up losing her store and caving in to his big business. That might be reality, but for me it's not a satisfying ending.

Sometimes the conflict is the characters themselves. Susan Elizabeth Phillips's books are incredibly dimensional because of the characters. She creates story people who are often ordinary and sometimes not even very likeable at the beginning, and then she makes them so interesting and real that we care about them and are invested in the outcome of the story. At the beginning of *It Had to Be You*, Phoebe Somerville is a bimbo and a troublemaker. It's downright crazy that her father left her a football team, and she hasn't the first clue about what to do with it, but she's determined enough to make it work. She instantly clashes with the team's head coach, Dan Calebow.

PHOEBE: "I guess we're like oil and water."
DAN: "I'd say we're more like gasoline and a blowtorch."

Underneath, Phoebe is vulnerable, an unwanted, unloved child who learns to love herself through the course of the story.

We can learn from Phillips that characters definitely don't have to be perfect—in fact, they shouldn't be perfect. If your hero is over the top with good qualities, he's not realistic. He needs somewhere to grow during the story, so you must make him a work in progress.

We sympathize with characters in conflict, especially if the conflict is of their own making and they're doing their best to change it. It's through their reactions to the conflict that we learn who these people are and see what they're truly made of. When we see them react, we learn something about them.

I teach this principle when instructing on synopsis writing, but it applies here as well:

> What the character is doing is not as important as why he is doing it. What's happening is not as important as how he reacts to what's happening.

Our characters have to face their worst fears. By the time that happens, we have shown the reader enough glimpses of their motivation to understand why they react the way they do.

STARTING YOUR STORY

It takes some thought to determine exactly where to start your story and integrate all the information you're preparing. I learned from Swain to start at the point of change. A couple of different schools of thought are taught, and you have to decide which one works for your story. One philosophy says we should see the main character in his normal world first, and sometimes that works. *Jerry Maguire* starts with Jerry's normal world. The point of change is when he writes his mission statement. The writers chose to show us his relationship with his fiancé and how he brags on the plane to give us a picture of his character before the point of change—a brilliant move.

Die Hard begins with John McClane boarding a plane on his way to see his estranged wife and kids for the holidays. He doesn't like flying, but he gets on the plane because he loves Holly and is hoping for the opportunity to work things out with her.

Another philosophy says to start midscene at a point of change, using dialogue, because this approach is fast paced and gets the reader right into the story. For me, personally, I am character driven—in reading, writing, or watching movies. If you show me a car blowing up in scene one, I don't care because I don't know anything about the people who were in it. But if you show me people interacting before one of them gets into the car, I am invested. Every episode of *CSI*, *Bones*, and *The Mentalist* briefly shows the soon-to-be dead or sick person in their everyday lives before catastrophe strikes. This invests the viewer in the outcome.

A great movie example is *Face/Off*. It's a fast-paced action movie, but it's also character driven. We are first shown John Travolta's character, Sean Archer, with his young son on a merry-go-round. Nicolas Cage's character, Castor Troy, while casually enjoying a soft drink, squints through his rifle scope and fires. The bullet goes clean through Archer and kills his young son. We care about Archer for the rest of the movie—we buy in because we saw that inciting incident. We can assume that the villain must have had a reason for wanting him dead, but now we know why Archer will do something as extreme as having his face changed via a revolutionary medical technique to catch the man who murdered his son.

When starting your story, consider how you want to present your characters: in their normal lives, before all hell breaks loose, or right in the middle of it.

EXERCISE

As you read or watch television or a movie, recognize the difference between conflict and delay in a plot. See if you can pinpoint the main character's goal, and write it down in one sentence. Then note the obstacles that keep her from reaching that goal.

[2]
MOTIVATION
AND REALISM

CHARACTER MOTIVATION

Nothing happens in a vacuum. People can't react without stimuli. Every action has a motivation—or it should.

You lean down and scratch your ankle. Why? It itched.

You go to the bank to make a payment. Why? You bought a car.

Your best friend bursts into tears. Why? Her boyfriend dumped her.

You gained five pounds. Um ... Snickers bars.

You ate too many Snickers. Why? Stress eating over the rash of burglaries on the news.

You buy additional locks and install them. Why? You can't afford another five pounds.

A man jumps every time a loud noise startles him. Why? Post-traumatic stress disorder.

A woman wants six children and a big house. Why? She grew up in an orphanage. Of course that's not the only reason a woman would want six children. She may have been raised in a big family and wants to continue as her parents and grandparents did. She could have watched too many misleading episodes of *The Brady Bunch*. Everything depends on her personality—and her motivation, backstory, and prime motivating factor.

A prime motivating factor or prime motivation is an event or a series of past happenings that shape a character's personality. In *Jaws* we saw the incident that shaped Quint's personality. Leonard Hofstadter on *The Big Bang Theory* is another character that comes to mind. When his mother is introduced on the show, she is almost a female replica of Sheldon, with a complete lack of social conventions, strict adherence to details, and an obsessive need for order, routine, and punctuality. Leonard admits to his neighbor Penny that as a child he built a hugging machine because he lacked love and affection. These over-the-top traits are fodder for comedy, but it's easy to understand how Leonard's character developed.

Some people whose parents are alcoholics adapt a similar lifestyle, and for them drinking is "normal." Others go to extremes to keep alcohol from their home. A woman who grows up in poverty may vow never to raise a child in that environment. She might refuse to have children until she's wealthy, or she may indulge them too much. Another woman might unconsciously hold back emotionally and financially from her child so he'll grow up as tough and capable as she did.

The really exciting part about creating characters is that you can manipulate their lives in order to tell the story you want to tell. That means you manipulate their histories to shape them into the people you want them to be so they react the way you need them to react. It's your job to make their behavior and reactions believable.

Create characters with built-in conflict.

Build in conflict as you personify your story people, and give them diversity. Use their pasts, their needs, and their fears as fodder for conflict. Use their strengths and their weaknesses *against* them. Their backstories, combined with characterization, will be motivation for everything they do. It will shape their goals and define the way they react to situations.

Weak, superficial motivations lead to weak, superficial conflict, which results in weak, superficial characters. Creating characters with embedded conflict from the planning stage will make your story strong and will ensure that you have enough conflict to carry the length of the book. Conflict that is superficial, external, or easily resolved will not sustain a plot. A cute premise makes for a great first meeting or introduction, but once that mistaken identity or initial problem is resolved, nothing is left to hold up the rest of the story.

I love to come up with an idea that seems impossible for the characters to overcome. If a situation looks impossible, it's a pretty good bet that the conflict will be strong. Occasionally I come up with something that looks so impossible that I have to put the idea on hold until I figure out a believable motivation and a resolution. A good example is my book about a large family who owns a brewery, *Her Colorado Man*.

My initial story idea was about a man arriving from a remote location and pretending to be my heroine's husband and the father of her child. I also wanted the man and the child to exchange letters before the man ever showed up. Why? Because that's the premise that stuck in my head and got me fired up. The problem was making the premise believable. I put this idea back on the shelf several times because I just couldn't bring it all together.

Obviously, the heroine would know this guy wasn't her husband or the father of her child—unless, of course, she had amnesia, and I wasn't going there. So in plotting this story, I had to motivate both of the characters to make this premise believable. Eventually it came to me: I gave the heroine a child with a secret father and a grandfather who made up a husband in order to protect her and their family name. The heroine is content to live her life pretending there is a husband off in the Alaskan gold fields.

However, unbeknownst to her, the grandfather used the name and post-office box of a real person. Wes Burrows gets caught in a bear trap while delivering mail in the Yukon and recuperates at the remote post office, where letters are piling up in his mailbox. An old man who used to read them and reply recently died. Because Wes was raised in an orphanage, the young boy's desire for a father strikes a chord in his heart, and he answers the letters. Eventually, he gets on a steamer and heads for the States to meet this boy and be a father to him.

You can see where this presents a big conflict for my heroine. Her family thinks Wes is really her husband, and now she has no choice but to let him into their family home—and pretend they're married. A lot of motivation planning went into making their actions believable to the reader. And this was definitely enough conflict to carry the length of the book. Marketing must have loved the premise because they sent out 750,000 sample packets of the first fifteen pages of this story in a reader mailing. I almost fell off my chair when I got that news. And reviewers specifically pointed out that they bought into the unlikely premise.

STICK TO YOUR GUNS

While writers must be open to change, suggestions, and new ideas, some factors should be considered sacred. I firmly believe this is critical to the plotting and brainstorming process. Before you ever brainstorm with another person or a critique group, lay down ground rules. Tell your partners the elements about the idea from which you will not budge—those things that got you excited about the story. Keeping these elements sacred is imperative. You need that seed of excitement to grow throughout the book. You must have that excitement when you reach the middle and require motivation to move forward. Never compromise the initial spark of creative genius that fired this story into being. If a story simply won't come together for whatever reason, shelve it for a later date. I've done exactly that many times. Nothing is lost by waiting. Trust me—much is gained.

Because of the conflict in that plot idea, I was able to draw emotions from the characters. A story is feelings, and if you plan your story to engage your character's emotions, you will engage your readers. It's our job to help them identify, show them why they should care, and then force them to buckle their seat belts and hold on for the journey.

Conflict reveals your character's emotions, and it's emotion through which your reader identifies. If the conflict isn't emotional for the character, it won't be emotional for the reader. If you want the reader to care about these people—*and you do*—engage his feelings.

In my novel *Her Wyoming Man*, courtesan Gabriella is pretending to be Ella, a mail-order bride from a finishing school. Nathan Lantry, an attorney who aspires to be governor, marries her upon her arrival.

> "You, Ella Lantry, are one of the smartest people I've ever met. You never judge anyone by their appearance or on a first impression. You are appreciative of the smallest thing, down to the most infinitesimal effort on another's part. You're quite curious. And you don't recognize your own value."
>
> A niggle of panic rose up inside Ella at his intuitive assessment. She couldn't afford for him to look at her too intimately. She swallowed to keep fear from her voice. "Well-read on the subject of explorers and wines doesn't mean smart."
>
> "I didn't say well educated, though you are. There's a difference. And I get the impression that you feel isolated, even here with our household or in a gathering."
>
> She didn't care for his shrewd perceptions, but she understood that they made him a good leader. "I admire you," she admitted. "And everything about you. Your honesty and your ambition and even your idealism."
>
> He raised his eyebrows. "Idealism?"
>
> "Yes." And more than anything she wanted to be worthy of such an upright and principled man. He was

as steady and unchanging as a rock in the middle of a raging river.

"No one has ever called me idealistic before."

"Perhaps I should stick to handsome."

He smiled, and this time it was a smile that crinkled his eyes and showed his teeth. He cupped her cheek and kissed her.

She liked everything about this man.

"This is new to me. Talking and enjoying each other, I mean. All along I was afraid to frighten you off. I didn't want to spoil what we had begun. Our marriage seemed so fragile."

It was more fragile than he imagined, but not for the reasons he thought. By taking this step and consummating their union, she hoped to strengthen their bond.

"Ella," he said, with an edge of seriousness that concerned her.

"You talk more than I might have anticipated," she said.

"I love you."

His words took her by surprise. *Love*? She blinked, hoping for comprehension. She threaded her hair back from her face without looking at him. "You didn't have to say that."

"No one ever has to say it. I told you because I felt it, and it was right to say so."

He loved her? Once she'd believed her mother had loved her, though, because the woman hadn't protected her from a life in the parlor house, she'd doubted her love, more now than even back then. After seeing children who were protected, she questioned what kind of love allowed a child to succumb to the fate Ella had. She'd seen the way Nathan safeguarded his children and planned for their futures. Her mother had never cared for her the same way. Of course the love he declared had nothing to do with parents and children. It was love between a man and a woman. No one had ever said those words to her before, and she didn't know how to receive them or to react.

He sat. "You don't have to say it," he told her. "I'm not expecting anything from you."

She recognized the pain in his voice, though. He wanted her to say it. "It's just …" she began and groped for words to explain. "I'm not sure I believe in that kind of love."

He was silent for a few minutes. The clock on the bureau ticked.

"You don't have to say it," he assured her. "But just so you know … I will make you believe."

Ella has never experienced a relationship other than one of servitude. Having been a prisoner her whole life, she has never enjoyed the most simple pleasures of everyday existence. Everything about her new life and the man who married her is unique and surprising. She can't reveal the shameful secrets of her past or she will lose this precious and tenuous new beginning. In this scene the reader sees Ella's well-protected vulnerability and recognizes that even though she wishes she could be honest with this man, her situation makes the truth impossible. The reader is experiencing this foreign concept of love along with her.

SIMPLE AND COMPLEX CONFLICTS

A simple conflict can be every bit as powerful as a complicated one; how the characters react and resolve it makes all the difference. A simple conflict relies more on internal conflict and characterization, while a complex conflict relies more on external conflict or plot.

The situation must be so important to the characters that it's intolerable unless they do something. You may have heard several of these terms, which basically cover the same thing:

- Motivation
- Backstory
- Prime motivating factor
- Prime motivating incident

This is the first sentence of the powerful prologue in Barbara Dawson Smith's *Fire on the Wind*: "Tonight his mother would finally love him." Seven-year-old Damien Coleridge garners all his courage to approach the mother who calls him a demon and a devil. He has spent hours on her Christmas gift—a picture he drew with scarred hands, which are a constant reminder of the fire two years previous that made his brother an invalid. His mother blames Damien for the harm to her favorite son.

While she's entertaining guests, Damien approaches his mother and accidentally breaks a vase, for which she verbally abuses him. He gives her the drawing. His mother takes him into another room where she tells him he's a devil who deserves to burn in the flames of hell. She rues the day he was born and wishes he had died. She throws his gift into the fire. That prime motivating incident drives Damien to spend his entire life living up to his mother's distorted opinion of him. He sees himself as totally unlovable. Her disgust and withheld love affects his every relationship from that moment forward. By knowing his vulnerability, the reader cringes when Damien faces rejection. Damien's internal conflict begins as a simple one and grows more complex as the plot develops over the years.

Your character's motivating factors don't have to be negative. He could be a person who can step in a steaming pile of doo-doo and come up smelling like freshly baked bread. You'd match this character with a jinx or an unlucky person. Or say your character had the perfect home life, with all the love and devotion a child could want. He believes in love and family, so you would pair him with a cynic and watch the fur fly.

When readers know about the experiences your characters have had, it makes the characters' goals and reactions motivated and believable.

Conflict must be personalized to the character. If you don't know your story people and motivate them, you won't have a strong conflict. A vague or general motivating force produces a vague and general plot. Being specific will increase the emotional intensity of your story.

DEVELOPING BACKSTORY

Everything that happened before the story starts is your character's backstory. Not all of it is interesting. Only a fraction of it needs to be revealed to the reader, and only the significant details are important to the plot.

When developing backstory, you will need to think about the prime motivating factors or the incidents that shaped your character. These are the memories you create for your story person and the basis for who they are now.

- **A BELIEF SYSTEM:** These are the precepts by which a person lives and may consist of faith, opinions on politics, philosophies, convictions, worldview, and ideals.
- **VALUES:** What is important to this person? Wisdom, skill, simplicity, reputation, order, independence, honor, freedom, discipline? Does your character look for the same values in others as in herself? By whose standards does she measure right and wrong?
- **FAMILY AND FRIENDS:** Family has fueled a good many plots and a lot of dysfunction, but family can also be held as a shining standard. Develop the history that results in the character you want.

- **FEARS AND PHOBIAS:** Some people are driven to succeed by fear, while others are crippled. What does your character avoid? What does she need to feel safe? Important? Loved?
- **PRIME MOTIVATING INCIDENT:** This is the factor that kicks the character into action in scene one.

In *One for the Money* by Janet Evanovich, Stephanie Plum loses her job as a lingerie salesperson at Macy's in Trenton and has her car repossessed. She needs a job. Her mother mentions her cousin Vinnie has a filing position in his bail-bond business, but instead of taking the job, Stephanie blackmails Vinnie into giving her a job going after people who've jumped bail. If she can get Joe Morelli to turn himself in, she could get $50,000. Stephanie and Joe have a history (backstory). When she was sixteen, she had sex with him in the bakery where she worked and he never called her. She later ran him over and broke his leg in three places, but she claims it was an accident. The conflict is built in and the story is set is motion.

It is imperative to keep your character's history in mind as you unfold the story. However, beginning writers often lay out all of their backstory right off the bat to make sure the reader gets it. Big mistake. This is known as an info dump. The reader doesn't care yet, so he's not invested for the time it takes to get through the backstory.

Remember to spoon-feed backstory: At first, simply *hint* at the inciting incident. A little later, taunt the reader with just enough to tantalize. Make him *want* to know, and then—when he *cares*, when he's wondering—let him have it with both barrels. I'll go into this in more depth in chapter 8 when I talk more specifically about characters.

EXERCISE

Take a look at the story you're currently writing or the one you're plotting. Consider your main characters individually. Using as few words as possible for each question, jot down the answers to these questions:

- What motivates your character?
- What inciting incident or factor in his past makes him the person he is today?
- What motivates his initial goal?
- What are the steps he will take to reach his goal?
- Do you need to adjust his backstory to motivate future behavior?

Look at motivating stimulus as your character sees it—with his background, attitudes, and knowledge. What's the worst environment in which you could place him? What would be a believable reaction to this setting or first scene? Turn up the heat!

[3]
AN EXPLICIT MISSION AND OPPOSITION

Movies to watch: *Jerry Maguire, Practical Magic*

Conflict is not a plot device—it's your character. When developing your character, make sure to explore and reveal the things that make this person who she is today. People aren't born as adults with personalities, likes and dislikes, phobias, and desires. Traits are created through years of life experiences, through childhood development, relationships with family and friends, and tests and trials. The fire of experience forges people into complex beings.

Know your character before you put words on paper. Know what she wants and why. Then tell her *no*. If your character is getting what she wants, you don't have a story.

CHARACTER GOALS

Conflict is divided into two separate but linked categories: internal and external (which I discuss in further detail in chapter 4). Many writers get confused over these two types of conflict, but neither is complicated. Both internal and external conflict must oppose the character's internal and external goals. Let's look at these goals first since you can't have conflict unless the character has something to oppose.

A goal is a mission. As stated in chapter 1, the character wants one of three things:

- Possession of something (girl, job, money)
- Relief from something (blackmail, poverty, abuse)
- Revenge for something (a slight, a loss, a betrayal)

We need to give our story people short-term goals and long-term goals. Short-term goals are decisions your character makes in order to achieve a long-term goal. For example, your character's long-term goal may be to win the Miss America Pageant. First, she must win the local pageant. In order to do that, she will have to buy clothing and take singing lessons. In order to do those things, she needs to raise the money. She must take many smaller steps to attain the larger goal.

All goals must be concrete and explicit.

My husband and I had boxes of movies on videotape, so we decided to watch and then get rid of them. One winter, we devoted our Sunday evenings to watching old movies before disposing of them. (Remember that movie watching is work if you're taking notes. You can learn more if you've already watched a movie at least once because if the movie is familiar, you can watch for character and conflict rather than waiting expectantly to see what's going to happen.) During our viewing sessions, we rewatched *Jerry Maguire*. The plot is a masterpiece, and the film is a great lesson in character goals.

Each character has a unique and concrete goal. Jerry's long-term goal is to be the best sports agent around. His short-term goals are to get clients and keep the one client he has—Rod Tidwell. His short-term goals will allow him to achieve his long-term goal.

Dorothy Boyd's goal is to be inspired, and Jerry inspires her with his mission statement. Her short-term goal is to make her decision work and make a go of working for Jerry. She's idealistic and needs to believe in the fairy tale. She also needs to take care of her young son.

Rod Tidwell, the football player, needs security for his family—that's his goal. To gain security he needs a new contract. He also wants professional respect.

Remember, conflict is opposition to a main character's goal, or the opposing goals of other characters. These opposing forces are derived from your characters. The stronger your character's goal and the stronger the danger that threatens it, the stronger your story is.

The external conflicts are easy to identify. Jerry's clients threaten to sign with another agent. One does. But his personal or internal conflicts are created from who he is as a person. Jerry believes he's sincere and that he devotes himself to relationships. He always asks, "What can I do for you?" as if he truly cares. But he hasn't really given his heart or soul to anything. Not to his ex-fiancé and not to his clients. Even after he marries Dorothy, he withholds his love.

Dorothy is driven by emotion and wants to love Jerry and see the fairy tale come true. She thinks if she loves him hard enough, their marriage will work. It doesn't happen that way. She recognizes and admits her flaws, though, something that takes Jerry longer to do.

Jerry tries to inspire Rod with hype, but Rod has a poor attitude toward the game. He saves his heart and soul for his wife and child. The theme of the movie is about giving heart and soul to everything. This is a good example of how conflict and theme are related.

Rod finally gives the game his all, and in doing so he inspires Jerry to give his heart to Dorothy.

SECONDARY CHARACTERS AND ANTAGONISTS

Once you know your main story people, develop secondary characters and villains to take advantage of their flaws and strengths. A villain also needs to be motivated. Sure, some villains are simply psychopaths, but a three-dimensional character can be scarier and more interesting. In *Jerry Maguire*, Bob Sugar has the same goal as Jerry—to get all the clients. Bob had been Jerry's mentor and taught him everything he knew. So why did we root for Jerry and not for Bob? Because Bob was all head and no heart. He personified Jerry's character flaw.

An opponent to be reckoned with is made all the stronger if he is personified. Your protagonists are only as strong as your villain or the problem. Therefore, motivate your villain. Make him believable. Just like your protagonist needs a flaw or two to round him out, a villain is all the more interesting if he's three-dimensional. The antagonists who evoke the most emotion are the ones who could have been heroes if they'd made better choices.

Conflict becomes motivation for the character's next decision and his new goal.

Conflict requires a decision; otherwise, the story doesn't go anywhere. When a character changes his goals, this prevents the middle of the book from sagging. The story will become static if we don't elevate the conflict and force the character to reevaluate his goals.

Conflict can be in the form of information. New information changes the character's goals and moves the story forward.

Types of new information:

- "You have a son."
- "You have six weeks to live."
- "I can't have children."
- Discovering someone's not really dead
- Uncovering a lie
- "You're adopted."
- "Luke, I am your father."

Sometimes new information is called a *reveal*, and it can change a plot from suspense to action. It might also bring up another set of questions. Luke now wonders if he will become like his father.

The following example is from my novel *Rain Shadow*.

RAIN SHADOW'S BACKGROUND: Rain Shadow was orphaned, adopted by a Lakota warrior, and raised in the transient lifestyle of the Wild West Show. As a young girl, a smooth *vaquero* left her pregnant and then married someone with respectability and money.

RAIN SHADOW'S INTERNAL GOALS: She desires to find out who she is and find a place where she belongs; she dreams of putting down roots and is determined to take care of herself and her son. She craves security and wants the respect that a heritage offers.

RAIN SHADOW'S INTERNAL CONFLICTS: She feels she doesn't belong in either world; she is out of place in Anton Neubauer's home, where her child is recuperating after a train derailment. Her son wants to stay, so she's torn between his happiness and her need to get away.

RAIN SHADOW'S EXTERNAL GOALS: She wants to be a champion sharpshooter because she believes that if she beats Annie Oakley, her real family will see her and come forward. She is determined to raise her son to be successful in the white man's world.

RAIN SHADOW'S EXTERNAL CONFLICTS: A train wreck keeps them on Anton's farm; she can't go on to winter quarters to practice; her son's father shows up.

ANTON'S BACKGROUND: Anton was married to a woman he didn't know how to relate to or how to please. His former wife withheld love and affection, though he tried his best to win her.

ANTON'S INTERNAL GOALS: He never wants to be vulnerable or hurt again and will never reveal his inadequacies or imperfections.

ANTON'S INTERNAL CONFLICTS: His son adores Rain Shadow. He feels a need to protect Rain Shadow and her son, and she doesn't need or want protection.

ANTON'S EXTERNAL GOALS: He wants to find his son a mother—someone for whom he has no feelings so he can't be hurt—to give his son two parents.

ANTON'S EXTERNAL CONFLICTS: The work resulting from the train wreck prevents him from proposing to another woman; both sons and fathers plot to keep Rain Shadow there.

As you can see from this example, the characters' internal and external conflicts are entwined.

Let's look at another great example. In *Practical Magic* a family of female magic-doers/herbalists have been cursed: The men they fall in love with are doomed to an untimely death.

Sandra Bullock's character is Sally Owens.

GOALS: Sally wants to live a blissfully normal life without magic. She vows never to fall in love.

MOTIVATION: As children Sally and her sister Gilly were taunted by townspeople. Now kids taunt Sally's daughters. She is motivated by her knowledge of and the results of the family curse.

CONFLICTS: Sally is a natural at magic. She has to do magic to help Gillian. She falls in love, not once, but twice.

Nicole Kidman's character is Gillian Owens.

> **GOALS:** Gillian wants to get away from town forever—she has to go where no one's heard of their family. Her deepest desire is to fall in love.
>
> **MOTIVATION:** Gilly has a minimal gift for magic. Growing up she was taunted for being a witch. Gilly is a thrill seeker.
>
> **CONFLICTS:** Gilly needs help to get away from abusive Jimmy Angelov. Jimmy tries to murder her, and Sally accidentally overdoses him.
>
> > **SALLY:** We have to go to the police. It was self-defense.
> >
> > **GILLY:** What, the old slowly-poisoning-him-to-death self-defense?

Aidan Quinn's character is Officer Gary Hallet.

> **GOALS:** Hallet's external goal is to find Jimmy Angelov's murderer. His internal goal is to find the woman whose letter he's read.
>
> **MOTIVATION:** He is an Arizona lawman; he fell in love with Sally through her letter to Gillian.
>
> **CONFLICT:** Officer Hallet loves Sally but suspects she's involved in Jimmy Angelov's disappearance/death. The sisters provide delay with a secretive cover-up. Jimmy comes back to life. (Now there's a problem!)

If you're looking at these elements and examples and thinking you'll never be able to pull a story together, you will. Once we understand the principles of story, the techniques are not difficult to put into practice. And everything takes practice. Remember, we have to be willing to write badly before we'll ever learn to write well. Learning comes from experience and trial and error.

In the last exercise, you listed goals for your main characters. Look at your list now. Have you listed concrete and explicit goals? Internal and external goals? Do internal goals stem from motivating factors in the character's backstory?

Next, look at two characters in your story:

- Write down each character's flaws and the emotional conflict that is keeping him from getting what he wants.
- Is there anything about the character's flaw that the villain (or other protagonist) can use to his advantage? Keep in mind that not every story has a villain. Sometimes your hero is her own worst enemy.

[4]
PLOT AND INTERNAL/ EXTERNAL CONFLICT

Movies to watch: *Runaway Bride*

WHAT EXACTLY IS PLOT?

I'm going to share something that took me forever to realize, but once I did, the knowledge set me free. Creating a plot sounds difficult. It seems difficult, and I used to think it was difficult. I had already written and published several books while believing that plotting was my weak spot before another light bulb came on and I understood how very uncomplicated plot is to define and construct. Once you understand the concept of conflict, you can create complex characters and believable plots. A poorly developed conflict is at most a reason for manuscript rejection and at the very least the basis for a lot of trouble when writing the middle and end of the story. It's better to get the plot right from the beginning, even if you need to tweak elements later. You can't write a book and then go back later and try to add conflict. It doesn't work that way because conflict is your characters. It's the skeleton on which you hang the muscle and flesh of your scenes.

So here's my epiphany, and I hope it's an eye-opener for you:

> Plot is the series of events that keep your characters together until issues are resolved at the end of the book.

When you look at it that simply, plot is not as intimidating as we make it.

Fiction is not real life. As soon as someone knows you're a writer, one of the first things you hear is, "You should write about my life," and then they want to jump in and tell you all about their horrible past relationship and their friend's dysfunctional marriage. As soon as any hint of "I've got a story for you," passes someone's lips, I hold up a hand to stop them and say, "The world isn't ready for your story." I don't bother to mention that the world will *never* be ready for their story because it has no structure. And though we say truth is stranger than fiction (and it may be) and real life can be fascinating, it isn't as marketable as a tale with a plot.

Great true stories like *The King's Speech* work because the truth contains all the elements of fiction: motivation, goal, conflict, disaster, black moment, and resolution. Most times, the writer or screenwriter embellishes and tweaks the true story to develop a workable plot.

I like a true story as much as the next person and I've read a lot of them, but they aren't fiction. Fiction has a structure that we must follow. Our story people must grow and change, but most importantly, they must be motivated.

INTERNAL AND EXTERNAL CONFLICT

Internal conflict is what gives the plot significance and keeps the characters emotionally at odds until the end of the book. It is based on ultimate desire and basic fear and stems from the backstory or the character's motivation. It prevents the characters from getting what they want and keeps the reader anticipating what will happen until the opposition can be overcome.

Weather, war, separations, sickness, accidents, travels—all of these are external conflicts. When they influence how the characters interact with each other and heighten tension between characters, they feed into the internal conflict.

Everybody wants something: safety, escape, comfort, power, shelter, social standing, knowledge, success, money, children, recognition, admiration, sex, love. All of these are external motivations.

The *reason* they want what they want—that's internal motivation.

Goal:	Motivation:
freedom	not enough self-confidence to commit
recognition	passed over for previous accomplishments
forgiveness	regain self-respect
peace	childhood was chaotic
riches	not lovable so must make oneself attractive
love	parent preferred another child
passion	raised in an emotionally sterile environment

The primary external motivation for every person is self-preservation, and the primary internal motivation is self-protection. Thus we often see heroes who have sworn to never love and be hurt again.

In *Runaway Bride*, Maggie Carpenter, played by Julia Roberts, fears losing her identity by getting emotionally involved with a man. In the past, every time she loved a man, her likes, dislikes, and desires became the same as his. Fear of losing herself took over, and she called off the wedding. Maggie's external goal is to go through with this current wedding. Her internal goal is to find someone to love. Her greatest fear is being alone. Her motivation was created by her mother's death and having to care for her alcoholic father. She equates love with selflessness and making the other person happy. Eventually, she has to confront her fears.

Ike Graham, played by Richard Gere, needs a good story to save his career. Ike's opposing external goal is to get the story when Maggie runs from the altar again. Ike's internal goal is to recover his inspiration and zeal. His greatest fear is vulnerability and heartbreak.

Reveal internal conflict as it's needed. Each time your character reacts to something, it shows the reader a little more about who she is. We sympathize with protagonists who face struggles we can understand, who must struggle to overcome an obstacle.

An interesting example of a sympathetic character is *Drop Dead Diva* on Lifetime. The real Jane Bingum is a young, gorgeous, skinny, blonde, self-involved shopaholic who wouldn't cut it as a sympathetic character. But when she suddenly dies and throws a hissy fit at the pearly gates, she pushes a button and ends up in the body of a plus-size, intelligent, successful attorney. Now this unsympathetic character is trapped inside a body that isn't hers, facing life from a whole new perspective—and she can't tell anyone. Her parents are divorcing, but since they don't recognize her, she can't communicate or express her feelings. She is forced to cope and change, and she becomes sympathetic.

CREATING A PLOT

Here is where plotting gets fun. You are the creator of your story universe. You are in control of past, present, and future, and you can manipulate it in any way that works to your story's advantage. You've got the power!

> Once you've given your story people motivation and goals, create scenes for them to react to.

Reacting to well-planned scenes makes the most of both internal and external conflicts. The most effective external conflicts are those you specifically create to feed into the internal conflict. This is why going back after the book is finished and trying to add conflict doesn't work—you haven't specifically created scenes with the purpose of seeing your character's desired reaction.

Remember the Indiana Jones series? In the first movie we learn that Indy has a fear of snakes, and then he's forced to jump into a pit full of them. We don't learn until *Indiana Jones and the Last Crusade* that as a youth he fell into a circus railcar filled with snakes—a prime motivating incident. At the end of *Raiders of the Lost Ark*, Indy has to overcome his fear to get the treasure and save the girl. These scenes would have been even more effective if we'd known his backstory up front instead of in a sequel.

In *Pretty Woman* Richard Gere's character has a fear of heights. Throughout the movie, he avoids the balcony at his hotel room, but at the end, he overcomes his fear to climb a ladder and propose to his love. A character must make a sacrifice in order to be truly heroic and show growth.

Internal conflict is what gives the plot significance and keeps the characters emotionally at odds until the end of the book.

External conflict can be used to keep characters together. External conflict does not keep characters apart emotionally.

With external conflict alone, nothing keeps the characters apart. *Romeo and Juliet* exemplifies external conflict. The characters are madly in love, and their families are the external conflict.

In *Romancing the Stone*, novelist Joan Wilder receives a treasure map from her recently murdered brother-in-law. Her sister is kidnapped, and the criminals demand she exchange the map for her sister's life. Ill-prepared, Joan sets out for Columbia, where she meets Jack T. Colton, a soldier of fortune who agrees to help her. Together they embark on an adventure. There is no backstory between them, no motivating factors to keep them apart emotionally. External events lead to mistrust, but external events aren't enough to keep them from falling for each other. In this example, external events keep them together. Internal conflicts are what push characters apart.

The characters in *Titanic* are kept apart because of external conflict. If Jack and Rose hadn't faced an iceberg, a sinking ship, or a mean fiancé, the story would have been pretty boring. The conflict of the sinking ship kept that story afloat (sorry, I couldn't resist). Still, they fell in love because there was no internal conflict keeping them apart.

AVOID EPISODIC EVENTS

Events lined up one after the other don't make a story. Events are given significance by how they affect the characters. Small annoyances, trivial events, or coincidences grow monotonous. These are examples of conflict for conflict's sake, and they will wear out or bore your reader.

► EXERCISE

Read a book or watch a movie, and make two lists, one of internal conflicts keeping the characters apart or causing them emotional distress and one of external conflicts keeping the characters from their goals. Take notes in your journal.

[5]
CHARACTER GOALS AND ORGANIZATION

Movie to watch: *Face/Off*

EVERY WRITER NEEDS A SYSTEM

I've shared a lot about how important it is that you develop your characters with conflict, know them well, motivate them, and make people care about them. Obviously, you're going to need a method to keep track of all of this information. Half of you will immediately say, "I can't plot or plan because I write by the seat of my pants." I get it; trust me. I started out writing 100 percent by the seat of my pants. Many of us do. But eventually, most of us realize that we can prevent a lot of mistakes and heartache with a minimal amount of planning.

Those of you who are on the opposite side of the spectrum, with color-coded index cards, lengthy outlines, and pages of character bios, character interviews, and storyboards ... as Donkey would say in *Shrek*, "Look at my eye twitchin'." But just because it doesn't work for me doesn't mean it's not the perfect system for you. Learn what system works best for you, and make the most of it.

You need a plan in place before you begin to write because you need to know where your story is headed. You're far better off with the assurance that your conflict will sustain the story. And eventually, you'll want to sell books based on a proposal. It's a rare author who doesn't have to write a synopsis, or at the very least a concept of her story, for an editor. And if you haven't already learned this, take my word for it:

> It's a whole lot easier to write a synopsis before a book is written.

Maybe embroider it on a pillow.

YOUR SYSTEM SHOULD WORK FOR YOU

You need a system for plotting your story. I can't tell you what will work for you. You will learn that from trial and error. But I can give you ideas and suggest you try them to see if they work for the way you think and write. We all create differently—don't ever let anyone tell you otherwise. It disturbs me when authors tell aspiring hopefuls that they have to follow a certain pattern or write a certain way or—I hate this one—that they must write every day. Yes, you have to write to get anything accomplished, but I take days off. Occasionally I plan a day off for mental and physical health. Scheduling other creative activities or time to simply not think at all may be just what's needed to boost your productivity the next time you do sit down to write. Have a schedule and stick to it, but allow time for life to happen. *Make* time for life to happen.

When I was a fledgling writer and heard "Real writers write every day," I took it to heart and spent a long time feeling inferior, like a fake writer, as if I wasn't as dedicated or as professional as others. But at some point I discovered a book called *Writing on Both Sides of the Brain* by Henriette Anne Klauser. The author tells the story of being a teacher and having a particular boy in her first-grade class who never participated or paid attention. For months she allowed him to walk around, play with things, devote his attentions elsewhere, and fail to turn in assignments, as long as he didn't disturb the rest of the class. She was frustrated and felt she wasn't getting through to this child. However, when the end of the term came and she asked if he'd like to tell a story and offered to write it down for him (she had begun to doubt he could even print), he grabbed the paper and wrote a story in cursive, using every technique she had taught—similes, metaphors, and alliteration! All that time he'd been processing her lessons with the luxury of silent time and no pressure to write. He went on to have a story accepted and published in a children's magazine.

That story set me free. I understand now that my time spent away from the keyboard is not unproductive. Now don't get me wrong—if you want to finish a book, you need to apply yourself to putting the words on paper. I'm a firm believer that you should finish every book you start. If you don't finish products, you'll never learn how to push past the middle or tie the end to the beginning or prove to yourself that you can follow through and be consistent. We all need to set deadlines and have strategic goals. But I don't believe everyone works the same way or dances to the same drum. Appreciate your differences. Use them to your advantage.

When I don't make time to do the things that rejuvenate and inspire me—call it the muse, if you will—I'm less creative and more apt to avoid the work or get stuck. Sometimes words flow for days on end. Sometimes they don't. It's okay to step back and fill the well.

It's wise to learn what works for you and then embrace it, as long as it's working. The same goes for story development, for how you store and access your research and plotting techniques. I get excited about a story by brainstorming, so I put a lot of energy into the process.

Goals, conflict, and motivation should be so specific that you can write them down in a few words.

You can go about this in a few different ways—or you can combine a couple of methods.

In the past I used a 5" × 8" index card for each character. As soon as I began to develop the story and the characters, I started filling out those cards. They helped me motivate my characters and gave me a map to consult when I needed help. You can develop these any way that works for you. Here's what mine held:

FRONT:

CHARACTER'S NAME:
INTERNAL GOAL:
EXTERNAL GOAL:
INTERNAL CONFLICT:
EXTERNAL CONFLICT:
How does the goal feed into the conflict?
MOTIVATION (FEEDS INTERNAL CONFLICT):

BACK:

FIRST CHARACTER TRAIT SHOWN:
STRONGEST CHARACTER TRAIT:
WEAKEST CHARACTER TRAIT:
SELF-CONCEPT:

```
WHY SHE WANTS TO (GOAL):
1.
2.
3.
WHAT SHE FEARS (WHATEVER SHE FEARS):
1.
2..
3.
HER COME-TO-REALIZE MOMENT:
```

Later, I copied the cards onto a sheet of paper and used that instead. Whatever works!

First Character Trait

I need to explain what I mean by "first character trait shown." When you bring your main characters on in their very first scene, on stage, so to speak, you must give readers the impression that you want them to grasp and carry throughout the rest of the book. Create the scene to do that job. You want your character to be sympathetic and likeable, but you also want to plant their most dominant trait in the reader's mind.

I mentioned the film *Face/Off* earlier. In the opening scene, the protagonist, Sean Archer, is playing with his little boy on the merry-go-round. They're smiling and having a good time together. Love is evident. While he's hugging his boy, he is shot by a sniper. The bullet goes clear through his back, exits his chest, and kills his son. The impression we have of Sean Archer throughout the rest of the movie is one of a loving, grieving father. This is a powerful setup and a strong motivating incident. The writer created that moment by bringing that character "on stage" with the character trait he wanted the viewer to hold throughout the rest of the story: a loving and adoring father.

The antagonist, Castor Troy, on the other hand, is casually drinking from a takeout cup while looking through his rifle scope. He knows full well that the child is there and in the FBI agent's arms. He's vividly portrayed as cold and calculating. The viewer immediately sees him as heartless. He carries that trait through the rest of the story.

You can also use index cards to list character traits that will serve as motivations. For example, my character Ruby Dearing in *Song of Home*, is rash, adventurous, audacious, stubborn, self-reliant, vulnerable, and a frustrated optimist. These traits affect her actions and reactions throughout the story.

When determining a list of character traits, ask yourself these questions:

- What does he need?
- Why can't he have it?
- What is his darkest secret?
- What is his ruling passion?
- What is his deepest regret?
- What is his dearest dream or fantasy?
- What does he want (love, success, freedom, security, etc.)?
- What does he avoid (rejection, fear, jealousy, etc.)?
- What is his strongest belief?
- What belief will change? Why?

Using index cards is only one way to develop your story. Study and learn the elements you need to know to flesh out your characters, develop an idea, and make a story work. That's what I've done, and I now have a surefire method that works for me.

THE BINDER OF WONDERS

As soon as I have an idea for a story, I write it down longhand. I write as much as I know about the characters and everything that excites me about the idea. Then I grab a binder and fill it with blank sheets of paper. Each book I write has its own three-ring binder. Writer friends who have seen these binders have affectionately dubbed them The Binders of Wonder.

This binder will hold all of my character grids, lists of names, research info, calendars for my timeline, maps, and a style sheet (which is a list of all proper names, places, people, streets, businesses, and so on). I also include writing-improvement articles that I plan to use as I write the book, as well as plastic sleeves for clippings and photos that might be useful.

Once my binder is ready, I develop a character prep sheet. I fill out one for each major character: hero, heroine, and villain, if I have one. If you like to use enneagrams (see chapter 27) you can jot down each character's contrasting traits and flaws. At the same time, I also make character pages.

For each character, I list the elements of story that help me create and sustain their conflict and bring it to a satisfying resolution:

- Name
- The inciting incident that kicks off the story, or the moment of change
- The character's motivation, prime motivating factors and incidents, what makes her who she is today and why she will react the way she does
- Her long-term goal(s)
- Her short-term goal(s)
- Character flaws and traits
- Internal conflict
- External conflict
- Black moment
- Character growth and realization, delivering on the promise in chapter 1

From these sheets alone, I can write my synopsis. I refer back to them over and over throughout the process of writing the book. They keep me on track, give me ideas, remind me where I'm going, and prompt me about the details I need to emphasize. They're the backbone around which my story fleshes out.

I don't have much use for character charts where you're supposed to fill out zodiac signs and physical characteristics and favorite foods and the names of their childhood pets. Those details are boring in real life; who cares about them with fictional characters? During story planning, the only time physical traits play a part is if they're inherent to the conflict. If you have a six-foot bruiser whose goal in life is to be a jockey, then he's got a problem. In one of my very early books, the heroine was over six feet tall, with freckles and orange-red hair. Her stepmother and half-sisters were delicate little creatures, and she felt like a giant among fairies. Insecurity over her physical appearance made up her internal conflict, so her appearance was important in the planning stages and the synopsis.

But if astrological traits and a list of favorite foods help *you* develop your characters, that's your method and I won't tell you it's wrong. Do it your way—but do it.

Think about the way you write and the things you have to know before you can sit down and start a book. I can't go forward without the perfect names and a title for the book. I know this is just the way it is for me, so names and a title are part of my brainstorming process.

To sum up: Keep up with your journal or notebook. It's a tool!

EXERCISE

Spend an hour prepping for a story you're working on or a story you're in the process of plotting. Make a storyboard using your scenes, or create a binder. Fill out note cards if they're helpful to your process. See if organization helps you feel more confident about what you're doing and about the direction your story is taking.

Watch the beginning of a few movies and/or read the first scene in a few books to see how the writer purposefully shaped your overall impression of the characters. Take detailed notes.

[6]
CONFLICT CHECKLIST

I write character-driven stories. Other writers are plot driven. No matter which kind of writer you are—or whether you're a plotter or you write by the seat of your pants (a "pantser")—you need conflict to drive your story.

I recently read the first three chapters from an aspiring writer's book that had been rejected. I could tell why the editor had returned the story as soon as the story people began bickering over inconsequential things. The writing was good and the characters were well drawn, but there was nothing substantial on which to hang the muscle and flesh of the story.

Yes, it's far easier to plan a book with conflict and *then* write it, but if you, like my friend, have already written a book and now recognize you don't have enough conflict, what can you do?

There are a couple of options. The easy one? Recognize that writing the book was a good learning experience, put it in a drawer, and start a new story. The difficult choice? See the areas that can be improved, be willing to ruthlessly get rid of what doesn't work, and add a skeleton framework after the fact. Difficult, yes, but not impossible.

Keep your tools at hand, and refer to them often. These tools are those you've chosen to plot your book, be they cards or an outline or character prep sheets.

External conflict is resolved before the internal conflict. By the end of your story, the character must have grown by continually changing his goals and his decisions up until that last and final decision is made.

Believable conflict that is worthy of strong sympathetic characters keeps your reader turning pages. The way you made her feel about your story makes her buy your next book. It takes planning and hard work to pull off a strong, emotionally charged book. It takes honesty and courage—and an amazing level of maturity—to look at your own work with an objective eye and see how you can make it better. It requires a desire to please readers and editors, as well as yourself, in order to be the best you can be. It takes a thick skin to acknowledge that not everyone will like your story or your writing, and it demands self-confidence to be okay with that.

A story is people we care about caught up in events that challenge their happiness (or their lives). There are only so many basic plots, but the amount of available characters and the ways you orchestrate their conflicts are limitless. You, the writer, are what make your story unique and individual and bring it to life in a way that only you can. Remind yourself often of what it was about this story that excited you. Brainstorm new ideas and possibilities. You are in control.

Above all else I remind you to write. Don't be afraid to make mistakes. Nobody walks before taking a few falls. No one learns to ride a bike by watching someone else or by talking about it or by reading books on balance. You have to get on the bike and give it a wobbly, sometimes scary shot before you can improve.

Don't look at unsalvageable manuscripts as a waste of time or an embarrassment. You learned what *not* to do, and that's a big accomplishment. If you have a stack of *completed* manuscripts, you taught yourself discipline. Pat yourself on the back!

I don't mind telling you I have half a dozen really bad manuscripts on a shelf in a storage room. And even after being published many times over, I still have several more unfinished proposals that never sold. The only reason my contract file is thicker than my rejection file is because contracts are twenty pages long.

But I learned. And I persisted. And I still learn and persist. I take online classes and listen to conference CDs, too. I don't know it all, but I continue to learn and seek knowledge.

We all need reminders to help us stay on track. I've developed this conflict checklist as a helpful guide and a prompt. If you're in the planning stages of your plot, use it as a guide to make sure you bring in the elements you need to create and sustain believable, solid conflict. When editing, ask yourself each question and decide how you can make the best use of motivations and reactions for emotional impact.

CONFLICT EDITING CHECKLIST

When plotting or editing, ask yourself these questions to make sure you've built a solid story:

- What is at stake, and is it important to the character?
- Is my character's goal obvious?
- Does my opening scene immediately engage the reader?
- How could this situation get worse?
- Could this conflict be easily resolved if the characters talked it over?
- Did I come up with unpredictable circumstances?
- Do I have time pressure?
- Does my character react according to his background/motivation?
- Do I have scenes of internal conflict?
- Why can't my character give up?
- What could happen to make the character change?
- Did the conflict create tension for one or more characters?
- Does the conflict force the character into action?
- Did I use scenes and viewpoint changes for tension and pacing?
- Are my characters a cast of diversified personalities who react to each other?
- What does the conflict make my character learn about himself?

GOAL, MOTIVATION, CONFLICT

Remember, your goal is to sell books. Your conflict, in the form of time restraint, family obligations, a real job, rejection, and so on, is your motivation for what you do next. Based on your character type and backstory, you will determine where you go from here. It's your decision.

PART TWO
ONCE MORE WITH FEELING

[7]
LEARNING
EMOTIONAL TRIGGERS

TONE AND ATMOSPHERE

When you meet a person for the first time, many factors shape how you feel about him, how you remember him, whether or not he makes a good impression, and whether or not you'd like to get to know him better. You can tell if a person is interested in you if they're listening to what you have to say. A good listener asks questions and isn't simply waiting for you to finish talking so he can insert his anecdote. The people we know and meet create emotional responses in us. The same goes for the books we read. What we take away from a reading experience is how it made us feel.

Get out one of your favorite books, one that sits on your "keeper" shelf. It can be an all-time favorite or a recent read. It should be one you can thumb through and find your favorite pages and passages.

Now take some time to think about the story. It would be a good idea to reread the book and recapture the feelings it created. Come up with an overall impression of the *atmosphere* of this story. How did the writing and the characters make you *feel*? You may remember an impression of intrigue or sexual tension. Perhaps a warm sense of family permeated the pages. The mystery of secrets or the thrill of suspense may have left an impression.

An *overall tone* is something you can't always find adequate words to explain. But if, when you think about the book, you remember the feeling you got from reading it, it was a *tone* that made an impression. And this story came to mind when I asked you to think of a favorite book.

My goal is for you to be able to open that book and recognize the word choices, descriptions, and dialogue that left such a strong and lasting imprint. As writers we convey impressions and images and feelings in one way only—through words.

In later chapters I'll discuss specific word choices.

LEARN WHAT TRIGGERS YOUR EMOTIONS

If available, buy a second copy of your favorite book—buy it used if need be. Use this study copy as a learning tool. I did this with many books when I was learning to write. Back then, I didn't have a network of writers or information at my fingertips. I read a lot of outdated how-to books from the library and did most of my studying by way of re-reading the books I loved. We can learn a lot from books we appreciate.

Use your extra copy like a textbook. Underline, make notes in the margins, and use highlighters to point out scenes where you reacted emotionally. Analyze what created those feelings: word choices, dialogue, body language, and character setup. The further we go through this section on feelings, the easier it will be for you to recognize those techniques.

Grab your notebook, and keep an emotion journal in one of the sections. Write down your thoughts and observations, and record the ways you see emotion conveyed and the things that make you react. Be alert during conversations with others. Watch television and movies with your eyes and ears tuned in to emotional triggers. Note your reactions and the reactions of others. Be observant. Note how setting creates mood and affects emotions.

You might even want to write down entire passages from other people's writing so you remember the things that moved you.

You must understand emotional triggers before you can write them with skill.

Observing what makes a good story and what triggers reactions is a key part of learning how to create those triggers in your own writing.

Your favorite authors have a unique way of triggering responses in you—and in a lot of other people. Most of those triggers are universal.

If you are obsessive—er, I mean a front-row student—and have access to a copy machine (one of the best investments I ever made, and they last forever; I'm only on my fourth), you might want to copy entire pages and scenes and keep a binder for study.

I said before that we learn best by discovering things on our own, so while I can point you in the right direction and suggest techniques, a lot of your learning will come from discovering things on your own, so be active in this process of learning what affects you emotionally.

FICTION IS DRAWN FROM REALITY

Emotion is scary, no doubt about it. Strong feelings make us vulnerable. At first, most of us are hesitant to let emotions bleed onto our pages. You might wonder if a parent will read this and think you're writing about them. You might hesitate because your friends or other writers will recognize something about your inner fears or vulnerability. If you write love scenes, you might be thinking about the people who will read them and wonder about their reactions. Will they think this is about you?

One of the most irritating questions writers can be asked is if we write from personal experience. Well, of course we write from personal experience! But do we experience and feel all the things that our characters experience and feel? Hardly. My answer is always, "My life is way too boring to write from personal experience."

I doubt anyone has asked Stephenie Meyer if she created a family of vampires from personal experience. Do we think Stephen King had a supernatural encounter in a deserted hotel or that he cut off his arm to see what phantom sensations were like? Seriously, people. We're writing fiction from our individual worldviews.

We become these story people, and we imagine what they would feel like or how they would behave given their background and experiences because we're creative and sensitive. We write from our deep creative wells of imagination, and we have lived and felt enough to be able to imagine how someone would feel in a given situation.

I have a dear friend who is a quadriplegic. I have no firsthand experience about what it's like to live life from a wheelchair, but Anita does. When I wrote *Sweet Annie*, I asked for her help, and she was a wonderful resource. Many years later, readers still comment about that story, and many say it's one of their favorite books. Why? I drew on people's emotions and made them feel what it was like to be Annie Sweetwater.

> Miss Marples' ice cream parlor wasn't very busy that afternoon, and the pudgy woman herself waited on them. After taking Charmaine's order, she asked, "And what will she have?" indicating Annie with a nod.
>
> "Well, I don't know, why don't you ask her?" Luke replied. "She's in a wheelchair, but she's not deaf or stupid."

This snip of dialogue is only part of what endears Luke to Annie and the reader. It would never have entered my mind to show Annie being treated like a nonentity in a scene, but because it's real life for my friend Anita, I was able to add more emotional depth.

Method Writing as a Tool

You don't have to have experienced something to imagine how it would feel. No one who sees an AMBER Alert has to question how the parents are feeling. That's a universal trigger.

One of the many things I do that drives my husband crazy is obsessively watching all the behind-the-scenes clips for movies. I know you've seen interviews with actors where they are talking about their character as though it's a real person. To them, it is. They become that person to take on the role.

It's method acting. It's how actors dredge up tears and show drama. They put themselves in that person's place and experience the scene as though it's happening to them. You have to know your character inside and out to write like this. Superficial writing will never convey deep emotion. You must first flesh these people out on paper and in your mind. Know everything you need to know about them. Give them backstory. Give them goals. These elements are all part of the complexity that makes up the creation of a story.

Use character charts or grids or interview your story people, but do whatever it takes to know them well. When you come to a scene of action or emotion, close your eyes. Think of the experiences this person has had. Let their life become real to you. *Become* them. This is how you will know how they will react and how they will feel.

I learned how to method write while working on one of my earliest books, *Rain Shadow*, in which two brothers were angry with each other. The particular scene just felt flat, but I didn't know why. So I closed my eyes at my desk and sat there, assuming all the experiences of the character in whose viewpoint I was writing. I felt angry about his situation, and my gut reaction—right or wrong—was to hit my brother. As soon as I had the character follow through on that and punch his brother, the whole scene fell into place. I had to become the character in order to understand his reactions to stimuli.

Did you know that *The Notebook* is the story of Nicholas Sparks's wife's grandparents? He has a very simplified writing style, but he reaches readers on a deeply emotional level, especially in that book, because the story was real. It was probably painful to write.

We all know what pain feels like. We've all lost someone or experienced rejection, and we've all laughed at inappropriate moments. We delve into our own emotions to write about feelings in fictional situations. We're human. Our readers are human. We connect through feelings. You're not writing an autobiography; you're tapping those core emotions as a resource for your characters.

One of your most beneficial learning tools, once it's developed, is the ability to understand—about yourself—what triggers your own strong emotions.

What works for you? Do you get weepy at Hallmark commercials? They are works of art in themselves, considering how few seconds the writers have to make an emotional impression and how well they do it.

If you're a comedy writer, what makes you laugh?

If you write in the thriller, mystery, or horror genres, what are your deepest fears?

When you know the answers to those questions, you know the kinds of books you should be writing, and you can learn to write using your strengths.

EXERCISES

Plop that favorite book on your desk or beside your comfy reading chair. Thumb through the pages; make notes in your notebook.

This week, watch your favorite television show and keep track of the dialogue, situations, and elements you find emotional.

You don't really need permission, but you have mine to watch as many movies as you like while discovering emotional triggers. If you get strange looks from anyone, explain that it's work! Keep taking notes. One of my notebooks is filled with pages titled "What Worked in [Title of Movie]." I make lists of the things that made the movie work for me. I went to see *Australia* three times in the theater, and then I bought it the day it came out on DVD. I didn't see *Avatar* as many times at the theater, but I did buy it on DVD and watched it repeatedly for a week.

Writers can't get too crazy. We can always say, "This is for an assignment," or, "I'm studying." See? Sounds convincing, doesn't it?

[8]
CHARACTERS
AND EMOTION

Movies to watch: *Pay It Forward, The Rock*

After you've thumbed through or reread your favorite book and made a list of the elements in the story that raised strong feelings in you, look over your observations. Did you watch any television shows or movies or read any books that touched you deeply? Did you recognize things that were intended to trigger emotional reactions? You probably discovered that the dialogue, situations, and events that triggered your emotional responses all came from your emotional investment in the characters.

If the reader doesn't care about your story people, he'll never make it past the opening scene or the first chapters. Characters make or break the story. Because I write a character-driven story, I rarely get through a talk or a workshop without emphasizing the importance of characterization, but even plot-driven stories must make the reader concerned about and invested in the outcome.

Ideally, you should have reread your favorite book by now and done a little thinking about why this story affects you the way it does. I can already tell you it's because you were involved with the characters and cared about what happened to them.

I've already explained the importance of building inherent conflict into the characters, but we also have to build in emotional involvement for the reader. If your heroine had a perfect childhood, was loved by everyone, got good grades, and sailed through to adulthood where she found a wonderful man, fell in love, married, and lived happily ever after, no one would care—or ever finish the book. Perfect and uneventful lives are boring.

We only have emotional responses when we feel strongly about something and when a lot is at stake.

CHARACTER MOTIVATION AND EMOTIONAL TRIGGERS

We're going to talk about motivation again—this time in regard to how it affects your readers' emotional triggers. Your character's motivation is what makes him believable. Each of your characters needs a prime motivating factor and a prime motivating incident. These are the experiences from the past that shaped them into the people they are today. Each one of us is the sum of our past experiences. Whether the experiences were good, bad, or indifferent and how we reacted to those situations influences how we think and what we say and do today. The reader can't have a strong emotional reaction if you don't set her up for one.

If the reader doesn't know who these people are, she doesn't care. If she doesn't know why the character acts and reacts the way he does, she doesn't care. Not caring is the kiss of death.

If your hero has an irrational fear of fire, we have a difficult time buying into it. But if you let us know that everyone he ever loved died in a fire, we understand his fear and overprotectiveness. We empathize with him. This is a man who will not readily run into a burning building to rescue the heroine. Behavior will seem irrational unless we know the motivation.

Your most important task is to *make the reader care.*

Remember, at the beginning of your story the reader hasn't had time to care yet. You're going to make her care. Telling all the backstory up front is like meeting someone for the first time who goes on and on about his mother-in-law's manipulation or relays their gallbladder surgery step by step. It's too much information, and you really don't want to know.

But if your best friend came over in tears and poured out all the details of her breakup, you'd be invested in the story and listen with both ears—and even comment! How dare he, that jerk? The difference is your involvement with the person. You care about your best friend. You feel her pain. When she cries, you want to hug her and take away her suffering. Quite a difference from the gabby stranger at the party, isn't it?

Up front, tell your reader directly what the character's goal is and how he thinks he's going to accomplish it. You may even state in one or two sentences why this goal is important. If Stanley Goodspeed doesn't get to the chemical-laden rockets on Alcatraz and diffuse them, General Francis X. Hummel is going to blow up a group of tourists and zap San Francisco, along with Stan's pregnant girlfriend. Now *that's* an emotional investment.

At the beginning of *The Rock*, we see Cage's character in his everyday environment, diffusing chemical bombs and then relaxing at home. His girlfriend tells him she's going to have a baby. As we digest this information and learn more about him, we care enough to be engaged in whether or not he gets a bomb dropped on him.

Unravel the backstory an inch at a time.

One of the most beautiful examples of unraveling backstory is in the movie *Pay It Forward*. If you've never seen it, please rent it now and study it for how character development, conflict, and even the setting make an impact on the story. I'll go into more detail in later chapters, because it's one of the most perfectly plotted movies I know.

The first time you mention major motivation, simply *hint* at the inciting incident. A little later, taunt the reader with just enough to tantalize. Make her *want* to know, and then—when she *cares*, when she's wondering—let her have. How do you go about doing that?

Let's examine *Pay It Forward*. Eugene Simonet's backstory is crucial to his character, but it isn't revealed until it's important to the other characters and to the story. This is a technique to hone: Make the other characters need to know what happened in the past—and make the reader *want* to know. In order for the reader to want to know, you first have to make her care. The scene that reveals Eugene's backstory is intensely emotional. He has been holding Arlene at arm's length, and because of her self-doubts and insecurities, she concludes it must be because she's not smart enough or not worthy. At one point early on, Trevor, Arlene's young son, asks Mr. Simonet what happened to his face. Eugene mistakenly thinks other kids put him up to it and sends him away. After Arlene and Eugene have been dating for quite a while, but Eugene still won't get close to her, she asks him if his problem is his burns and adds, "If that's even what they are. Is that what they are?" to which he replies, "Yes." That's well over halfway through the movie, and he's still holding back about his backstory. Arlene can't figure him out. She feels rejected. The viewer can't figure him out either, but boy, do we want to know! Eventually he lets her see all of his scars but explains nothing.

Arlene's ex returns. Eugene withdraws, but Arlene confronts him and tries to explain why she is giving her abusive ex another chance. And then, while Arlene is now dreading the truth and the viewer is holding her breath, Eugene tells the horrendous story of how he got those burns. This is what we want to do in our stories: We want to wait until it's important to the others characters and to the reader before we reveal everything.

CONNECTED BY THEME

All the characters in *Pay It Forward* are connected by a theme: "Can one person make the world a better place?" Keep in mind I've chosen movies and books because of specific elements and how perfectly they exemplify a point. Certainly it would be ideal to have every character in a book connected to the theme, but it's not always realistic or even possible. It is a good idea to pinpoint a theme for your story. It will help with cohesiveness and later on with your blurbs and book descriptions.

CRAFTING BELIEVABLE CHARACTERS

Showing how the character perceives the world makes him unique and believable. It's also part of the writer's voice for the story. How the character perceives *himself* is equally important. Your story person must be someone with whom the reader can identify. They don't have to be extraordinary because ordinary people facing extraordinary circumstances are often more interesting.

Let your characters have insecurities. Your main character should be someone the reader could imagine being or knowing.

Secondary characters must be credible, too. They should portray someone who could be your grandmother, the old man next door, a teacher, or a neighbor—in other words, real people, people you would like to know or who have personalities that remind you of someone.

This goes for physical attributes, too. If the heroine thinks of herself as exquisite and beautiful, she's probably not someone we'd like to be friends with. Besides, those are usually point-of-view issues: In real life a person wouldn't look in the mirror and think that her lips are shaped like rosebuds. More likely, like Stephanie Plum, she would look in the mirror and think her hair looks like a Brillo pad. It's best to let other characters make observations about your protagonist while you're in their heads.

The most efficient way to write a walk-on character is to use stereotypes, because the reader already has an impression. This, of course, depends on the length of your story and the importance of the character.

In summation, you must deliberately create sympathetic and believable characters in order to create an emotional response in your reader. In the following chapters, I'll share techniques to help you do just that.

In your notebook, write down the highlights of your character's backstory.

- Is there an incident that affected how he views himself?
- Did something shape his childhood or incite him to feel a particular way?
- Who had the greatest impact on him?
- What prompted him to embark on his present career?
- How does he feel about the opposite sex, politics, religion, children, and the environment?
- How would he describe himself?

Did you already know the answers to these questions, or did they provoke you to come up with something you were unaware of until now?

How can you use these incidents to your advantage in the story?

[9]
INTERNAL NARRATIVE AND DEEP POINT OF VIEW

If you've been making lists in your notebook, watching movies, reading, and analyzing the triggers that create strong emotion, you should have a grasp of how to create strong emotion in your own stories. Let's say you've given your character a fantastic motivation and a detailed backstory and have an idea about where you're going with this story. How are you going to draw emotion from your reader now?

One of the ways to do this is with internal narrative—your character's thoughts. What your character is thinking defines her as a person and makes her either sympathetic or unsympathetic. Everything your character thinks will affect how your reader perceives her, so choose carefully.

In this example, a man wants a woman to set aside her plans and go camping with him for the weekend. Here are two different scenarios:

> **FIRST SCENARIO:** He hoped Susan would be willing to leave the city behind for a couple of days and join him on the river. It had become more and more obvious that she needed some separation from the situation. He had the means … and the inclination, so why not make the offer? If she said no, at least he'd have tried. If she accepted, he'd be a happy man. It had been too long since he'd seen her smile.

SECOND SCENARIO: He put in the last bag of groceries and shut the trunk lid. The wine had been a nice touch. Never hurt to deaden a few inhibitions. Smiling to himself, he started the car and headed for Susan's office building. Women were like puppies. All he had to do was play nice with her, keep her fed, and she'd follow him wherever he led. This weekend all roads were leading to his cabin. She'd be eating out of his hand by Sunday morning.

Which man is more likeable?

Your opinions of each man are based on what they were thinking for a few brief seconds, but it made all the difference in how you felt about them.

Your character's thoughts are going to show her growth throughout the story as well. She's going to learn something or come to terms with something or solve an attitude problem by the time the story ends.

SCENE AND SEQUEL

Internal narrative is used throughout your story. It's what your characters are thinking and how they react to stimuli. Your characters' thoughts can be used in scenes and are effective in sequels. In their books on writing, Jack Bickham and Dwight V. Swain explain the concept of scene and sequel as presenting a scene of action and then a scene of reaction, one after the other, like a chain of links. For example, in a scene, three people witness a crime and are discovered, so they run. In a sequel, they stop and decide whether or not to go to the police and how to protect themselves.

SCENE OF ACTION: Something is happening, like a conversation or an alien attack or a bank robbery. New information may be revealed in scene or something can be discovered. A kiss is a scene. A conversation is a scene.

SEQUEL: Your point-of-view character thinks about what just happened, analyzes it, and makes a decision about how to move forward.

In *Writing the Breakout Novel,* agent Donald Maass suggests that sequels are old fashioned and unnecessary in today's market of fast-paced fiction and modern fiction-writing trends are beginning to reflect this. Fewer and fewer books are written with scene and sequel neatly segregated, and fiction, like the movies, is more fast-paced than it was twenty or thirty years ago. I appreciate Maass's observation, though I haven't done away with sequels entirely because I think it's important to show what the character is thinking and how they're reacting to the scene. I tend to include my sequel within the scene as it's happening or at the beginning of the next scene. This means that while an event is happening, my character is reacting to it and thinking about it. And he might think about it later, too.

In a scene from my book *Saint or Sinner,* the male protagonist learns stunning information and reacts at the same time.

> Joshua stared at her for a full minute. Her agonized eyes never left his. Surely the information would sink in and make some sense. At a loss, he repeated her words. "The Reverend Picker is your father."
>
> Her lip quivered and a mere whisper escaped. "Yes." Finally, she looked away.
>
> "Addie." He took her hand. "Are you saying that he's the person who did this to you?"
>
> "Yoo."
>
> "Are you quite sure?"
>
> "Yes."
>
> His disbelief must have sounded in his voice.
>
> "Why?" was all he could think to ask. The reverend was her father, but he'd beaten her almost to death.
>
> "He wanted the money," she said simply.

"That bag that was beneath your skirt." Her trembling fingers were cold, and he rubbed them between his palms.

"He took that," she said, and when she went on, her voice shook as much as her hand. "But he wanted the rest of it. The money I put in Mr. Latimer's safe."

Vaguely now, Joshua remembered her saying she wasn't comfortable with all that money and wanted to place it in the bank.

"He's not what you think he is," she said. "He came to Van Caster for one reason. To take people's money. And I knew." Plump tears formed in her eyes. "I knew, but I was too much of a coward to do anything about it. I thought if I just kept the money in a safe place, so he couldn't get to it, it would be all right."

Guilt and remorse were etched on her battered face. "I'm sorry," she whispered brokenly. "I'm so sorry. I ran away from him before I came here," she confessed. "I had to. He'd ... done th-this to me before."

Some of the initial shock was starting to wear off. Joshua fitted pieces of the puzzle together. *People aren't always what they seem*, she'd said to him that night as she'd tended his head and put him to bed. There'd been layers and layers of meaning in those few simple words. *You don't know me*, she'd told him.

She set such store by having everything in order and on schedule. Order was a security she created for herself. She'd never played horseshoes or taken Sunday dinner with family. She'd rejected his proposal because they were too different.

Emotions warred within his breast. *Too different.* Like a bubble rising to the surface, the thought came: He'd fleetingly wondered why she owned face powder. *Addie was used to covering bruises. ...*

The man's words, when he preached, had never lain quite right on Joshua's heart. The first time they'd passed the revival wagon on the road, she'd had an odd reaction when the two youngsters had waved to them.

"The boy and girl who take the offerings?" he wondered aloud.

"My brother and sister, Miriam and Aaron," she responded gravely. "Miriam and I were meeting at the church. I was going to take her with me this time."

She'd said she couldn't marry him because she might not be here much longer. She'd been planning to run.

Inside, Joshua seethed. He'd controlled these emotions for days now. With no one to fix them on, they'd rolled and burned. Now that he knew who had done this to her, his first thought was to find the man and kill him.

He bolted to his feet.

We must give our characters strong motive to react, and then we must show them reacting without slowing down the story or bringing it to a screeching halt by going into page after page of thought, internal narrative, deep point of view, or reaction.

Your character needs to be reacting to what's going on around him. He needs to be thinking interesting things that characterize or move the story forward. At the end of the book, one or more of your characters must think about what they've learned and the price of either reaching their goal or forfeiting it.

A story is a series of stimuli and reaction. Every reaction is different based on past experience. Never miss an opportunity to show a character's reaction. Never have something happen without motivation. If you're going to point out a beautiful horse or a sunset, show your character reacting to it.

DEEP POINT OF VIEW

Using the character as the story's camera and filter and monitoring their feelings and thoughts firsthand as they happen is deep point of view. It allows the reader to become the character and live and breathe in their shoes. I hadn't heard the term until several years ago, but I instinctively knew what the technique was and had already been using deep point of view. A recurring mistake I see beginning writers make is jerking the reader out of the narrative with words that remind her that someone wrote this story. We don't want to point out to the reader that she's not experiencing the events firsthand. You, the writer, want to be invisible. You don't want to write flowery prose or use words that distract the reader from becoming immersed in the narrative.

Here are attributions and phrases that jerk the reader out of the character's head:

- "he thought"
- "she wondered"
- "she saw"
- "she heard"
- "he believed"
- "he realized"
- "she decided"
- "she wished"
- "he remembered"
- "her thoughts wandered to…"
- "he thought to himself" (This is one of the worst offenders— who else would he think to?)
- "you" sentences: "It was a burden, like the kind you carry for years."
- excessive italics or underlining

I've seen suspense or mystery novels present huge passages of the villain's internal narrative using italics or underlining to great effect—however, even that can be irritating and might be just as effective presented in plain text. As a general rule, use italics sparingly, a few times per chapter perhaps.

Don't tell the reader that the character is thinking—just have the character think it.

For example, instead of:

> He thought Gizmo was the funniest looking dog he'd
> ever seen.

Deep point of view is:

> Gizmo was the funniest looking dog he'd ever seen.

If you write internal narrative effectively, you don't need to use attributions as though the sentences were dialogue, such as *he thought, she wondered*, and so on.

> He wondered where she'd hidden the deed to the house.
> He believed it was probably hidden in that old trunk up-
> stairs. Travis saw several photographs on the table as
> he passed through the kitchen, and he picked up one.
> It was a picture of the two of them, taken the summer
> they'd rented the house on the lake. She was smiling at
> him the way she used to.

There are a lot of things wrong with that paragraph. First of all, I don't have to tell the reader that Travis is wondering or thinking or believing if I simply get into his head and show the story through his eyes and viewpoint.

> Where in blazes had she stashed the deed? Lydia's
> predictability was one of the things he'd always loved
> about her. She kept everything from old cancelled checks
> to her birth certificate in that trunk upstairs. On his way
> through the dining room, a scattered pile of photos cap-
> tured his attention. He recognized the one on top before
> he even picked it up and held it to the late afternoon light

> slanting through the blinds. That summer they'd spent at
> the lake had been one of the best times of his life. Back
> then they'd still smiled at each other like silly teenagers,
> still held hands on the beach ... still had dreams.

See the difference? In the first paragraph, I pointed out that Travis was thinking those things and I told you what he was doing. In the second paragraph, I *became* Travis (method writing) and experienced the scene through his eyes, with his backstory as motivation. You don't even have to know his backstory to know he and Lydia are not on good terms now and that he has strong feelings about both their past and present relationship.

If you wanted to add something immediate and stronger for more effect, you could do this:

> Back then they'd still smiled at each other like silly teen-
> agers, still held hands on the beach ... still had dreams.
> *I can't go on like this.*

The switch to first person is smooth, brief, and perfectly fitting for the scene. It's more seamless to stay in third person:

> Back then they'd still smiled at each other like silly teen-
> agers, still held hands on the beach ... still had dreams.
> He couldn't go on like this.

Stephen King excels at deep point of view. That's why we are always hooked from page 1. That's why we were terrified by *The Shining*. In this passage he uses vivid words, like the "tumble of his thoughts," the "soft and futile sound of the doorknob" turning, the shrieking storm, and his "feet whispering" on the carpet to bring us squarely into Jack's immediate reactions. "If he opened his eyes and saw that doorknob moving he would go mad" keeps us in Jack's head, experiencing fear with him.

> "No," he whimpered, hardly aware that he had been re-
> duced to this, whimpering with his eyes shut like a child.
> "Oh no, God. Please, God, no."

But below the tumble of his chaotic thoughts, below the trip hammer beat of his heart, he could hear the soft and futile sound of the doorknob being turned to and fro as something locked in tried helplessly to get out, something that wanted to meet him, something that would like to be introduced to his family as the storm shrieked around them and white daylight became black night. If he opened his eyes and saw that doorknob moving he would go mad. So he kept them shut, and after an unknown time, there was stillness.

Jack forced himself to open his eyes, half-convinced that when he did, she would be standing before him. But the hall was empty.

He felt watched just the same.

He looked at the peephole in the center of the door and wondered what would happen if he approached it, stared into it. What would he be eyeball to eyeball with?

His feet were moving.

(feets don't fail me now)

Before he realized it. He turned them away from the door and walked down the main hall, his feet whispering on the blue-black jungle carpet. He stopped halfway to the stairs and looked at the fire extinguisher. He thought that the folds of canvas were arranged in a slightly different manner. And he was quite sure the brass nozzle had been pointing toward the elevator when he came up the hall. Now it was pointing the other way.

"I didn't see that at all," Jack Torrence said quite clearly.

But he didn't take the elevator back down. It was too much like an open mouth. Too much by half. He took the stairs.

Create the character's thoughts to match their speech, intellect, upbringing, ethnicity, regional phrases, and personality. A child will think like a child. An uneducated man will think like an uneducated man. A stuck-up snob will think like a stuck-up snob. You get the drift. Your characters' thoughts shouldn't sound like *you*. Developing unique voices for them takes forethought and practice.

Here's an excerpt from *Land of Dreams* where I use the viewpoint of a young boy with little education who is running from yet another abusive situation:

> A cup landed in his plate, splattering his last few beans on his already stained shirtfront. "Wake up, slum boy! Clean them dishes. There's cows to milk."
>
> Lucas glared hatred at the man. "I was still eatin'."
>
> "Don't back talk me, boy! You was dreamin'. Like yer always dreamin' 'stead o' workin'. I feed you, and you try to get out o' workin'."
>
> Lucas stared back, wishing the hateful man dead.
>
> Bard yanked an ax from a makeshift cupboard and disappeared through the open door.
>
> The scarred tabletop blurred. Lucas concentrated on the aged ring burned into the wood until his vision cleared. This wasn't the worst place he'd ever lived, but it was close. The man had lied about having a wife at home. And heaven only knew where he'd found references for the agent. Lucas could tolerate the bedbugs that chewed him alive at night. He could endure the endless meals of beans and salt pork and dry biscuits. He could even tell himself this snake-infested hole was better than the garbage-filled alleys of New York.
>
> What he couldn't abide was that crude, smelly man. Gophertown, he'd heard some of the townspeople call this section; Gophertown, because the occupants lived in holes dug into the side of a hill. Bard belonged in a hole,

Lucas was convinced. However, the hole should have been six feet deep and then filled with dirt.

"You lazy, good for nothin' alley rat!" Bard shouted from the doorway, and Lucas jumped, falling backward off the crate.

Buttocks stinging, he leapt to his feet.

"I knew you wasn't doin' them dishes. You got to be watched ever' minute!" Bard flexed the leather razor strap between both fists, leveled his rheumy gaze and stalked him.

Lucas was lighter and faster, and he escaped Bard's first clumsy attempts. Dodging and darting in the darkness, he tripped over a stool and fell to the hard-packed dirt floor with a grunt.

Everything that happens in this scene is immediate, and Lucas is the camera and filter for the action. He reacts to the stimuli the way an untrusting young boy would, instinctively and self-protectively. The reader is able to experience the action with him because of deep point of view and reactions.

We get to know a character well because we spend time in his head. As the author it's our job to show opinions, descriptions, likes, and reactions through their thoughts. We become the character and use deep point of view to let the reader in on the character's deepest musings—the things he would never actually say aloud.

EXERCISE

Write a few paragraphs in the deep point of view of one of your characters. Show emotion through a reaction without using any of the aforementioned attributes, like "he thought" or "she wondered."

[10]
WORD PICTURES AND DIGGING MORE DEEPLY

"Lacking emotional punch" is a buzz phrase editors often use when rejecting manuscripts. I have never received this reason for rejection, so hopefully I have the "emotional punch" thing down, but for other writers, "emotional punch" may be more elusive. My critique partners kid me about loving angst, and I do—at least in stories and movies. I mentioned before that not every story has to be angst ridden and not every cast of characters needs horrible backstories, but every story *does* need to strike a chord with readers.

Why does Janet Evanovich's Stephanie Plum appeal so much to us? We laugh at her trials and antics, but we relate to her. She's the frizzy-haired klutz we all felt like in junior high. Her family drives her crazy, but she loves them and they love her. She drives a heap of junk and is often just a few minutes late for the good evidence, but she's right on time for bad things to happen. It's because of all these things that she's believable, and we want to root for her and can picture ourselves in her place.

The Stephen King example in the previous chapter was chock-full of vivid word pictures. Descriptive words that form pictures in our minds help us connect. Word pictures evoke emotion with which we can easily identify.

A story without strong emotion is not a story brought to life. Editors are looking for depth and color and fire. They're looking for those emotional connections that will make readers remember the book long after they've read the last page.

We can use certain character types, traits, and situations to automatically create sympathy or evoke other strong feelings. I call these factors *givens*. Laugh if you will, but babies, cowboys, and virgins come with ready-made feelings, and that's why they appear on the covers and in the pages of so many category books. These elements sell books. Any number of givens come with automatic reactions: widows, divorcees, children, dogs and other animals, orphans, stepmothers and stepfathers, victims, military men and women, sacrifice, bravery, the death of a parent ... and the list goes on.

But simply using a given on its own isn't effective unless you motivate all the characters to care and react. I often cite Stephen King's works because he is a master at using childhood fears and other triggers to make his characters sympathetic and engage the reader. The unknown is always frightening, but it's even worse when it's that unknown thing in the closet, as in *Cujo*. The novel *Carrie* is fueled by adolescent alienation and embarrassment—things we can all relate to. King uses vivid descriptive words to evoke mental pictures and feelings in this passage from *Pet Sematary*:

> He grabbed Church [the cat] and draped it over his arm— he didn't bother much with the broom these days. He supposed that, in spite of everything, he had almost gotten used to the cat again. He went toward the entryway door, turning off lights as he went. When he opened the door communicating between the kitchen and garage, an eddy of cold air swirled around his ankles.
>
> "Have a merry Christmas, Ch—"
>
> He broke off. Lying on the welcome mat was a dead crow. Its head was mangled. One wing had been ripped off and lay behind the body like a charred piece of paper. Church immediately squirmed out of Louis's arms and nuzzled the frozen corpse eagerly.

I'll spare you the rest of the paragraph describing what the cat does with the body of the crow. But you can see how vivid words create powerful images.

The way you set up a character generates emotion for your reader, and the manner in which you lead the reader through a scene evokes feelings. Invest the reader in the scene by playing into those things that trigger strong reactions.

This is the opening scene from my book *Prairie Wife*:

> Amy would never know how many shovelfuls of earth it took to fill a grave so heartbreakingly deep and yet so pathetically small. She'd lost count around two hundred or so. The first falls of dirt had been loud, landing on the sanded and varnished wood coffin with a mind-numbing thud.
>
> A couple of women had urged her away from the grave, but she'd resisted their efforts and had remained to experience the entire ordeal. It was the least she could do. Jesse had built the casket. A day and a half it had taken him. A day and a half while she sat beside the small, still body laid out on wooden planks in the dining room, barely acknowledging visitors, gifts of food or expressions of sympathy. The finished project, when he'd carried it into the house, was a work of art. An eloquent expression of love and grief. An outpouring of everything he felt and could express only in this final gesture for his son.
>
> Amy had left the room while Jesse and her father, Sam Burnham, placed the lifeless body of her barely three-year-old child in the casket. When she'd returned half an hour later, Tim looked as though he were merely sleeping upon the luxurious fabric. He looked as though at any moment, his eyelashes would flutter and his blue

eyes would open; he'd smile that smile that touched every place in her heart and left her aching with pride and love.

But Tim was as still as he had been since she had pulled him from the creek behind the station and tried to breathe life back into him. He wore his Sunday clothing, dark pants and a white shirt, a miniature string tie. His fair hair was neatly combed, and the obstinate curl that had always fallen over his forehead had been tamed into perfection.

As Amy watched, Jesse ruffled the lock so that it fell upon Tim's forehead in the endearing way it always did. She knew just how soft Tim's hair felt beneath Jesse's loving touch. She had finger-combed it back a thousand times.

Taking a step closer, Amy noticed something in Tim's hand that hadn't been there before. A ray of sunlight streaming through the dining room window glimmered on gold. Her boy held a watch. The pocket watch that Jesse's father had given him, and with which Tim had always loved to play. As a baby, he'd sat on Jesse's lap, enthralled with the timepiece. Jesse had promised the child that one day the watch would be his. It shouldn't have been so soon ... and it should never have been like this. ...

The watch's *tick* was loud in the silent room. The sun caught and reflected droplets on Tim's still tiny hands. Tears. Tears had fallen from Jesse's eyes, tears were still streaking her husband's lean cheeks

As if in a cocoon of silent unreality, Amy watched without feeling anything. The place where her heart had been was a cavity. Cold. Empty. Jesse had carried on. Jesse had built a coffin. Jesse ate and drank coffee. Jesse *cried*.

Amy was as lifeless as their son.

The least she could do was stand here now and watch it all. Watch as her father and Jesse scooped dirt and moved it into the grave, their shirts growing damp with sweat. It must feel better to do something. But she didn't have to feel at all, did she? Everything would be okay—she could survive without letting out the scream on the inside.

Jesse paused in his efforts to wipe perspiration from his eyes. Perspiration—or tears? His blue gaze lifted and discovered her standing across from him. If there was a message in his expression, she didn't receive it. He had tried to hold her the night before, but she'd turned away, unable to allow him into her private world of nothingness.

Amy closed her eyes and thought of her precious Tim in his little shirt and pants, lying against the blue velvet. Thought of the watch ticking ... ticking ... until it wound down ... silent forever. Like her son.

I didn't write any dialogue in this scene, which is unusual for an opening. The lack of speech shows Amy's inability to express her feelings or communicate, and this inability is a thread of conflict throughout the story. My decision to show her internal thoughts first brings her on stage "in character." The lack of dialogue also lets the reader experience the moment right along with Amy in her silent misery. Amy hears the dirt thudding on the coffin and the tick of the pocket watch, and the reader reacts. Descriptive writing is more than visual; it employs all the senses.

This scene was written in deep point of view to show Amy's experience firsthand, to evoke emotion and involve readers. We want to draw emotion from readers, not beat them over the head with it. Melodrama is not effective. Amy watches her husband's emotional reactions as if from afar because she's distancing herself from the pain she's unable to let herself feel. The point of this scene is to involve readers in Amy's paralyzing grief without *telling* them what Amy is feeling or *telling* them what to feel.

Never be afraid to dig into your character's head and heart and pull up emotions and thoughts that are difficult to experience. You can't grab your reader if you remain on the surface. You should feel right along with your character. If it's funny to you, it's funny to them. If it makes you cry, it makes them cry. To keep it interesting, go beyond your gut reaction.

I often find myself pausing to think as I'm writing a scene. I certainly advocate spontaneity to create honesty of voice, but stopping to consider all your options for how to present a scene and to think past the obvious will always bring out a deeper reaction, a stronger emotion, or a better, more original phrase. Sometimes as I'm writing narrative, I stop and ask myself, "Would this scene be more effective as dialogue?" Sure enough, the same words spoken by the character often create a stronger scene and provoke a stronger reaction from the reader.

Look past the initial reaction and emotion, remembering anger is a secondary emotion. Your story person is royally ticked off, but why? What's beneath that anger? Get to the core problem. Don't use abstract expressions; be explicit with words.

In the next chapter, I'll outline the film *Pay It Forward*. You'll get more from this chapter if you watch the movie beforehand.

EXERCISES

Create a list of givens you're using in your story. Is there universal appeal?

While working on your story, write several paragraphs using word pictures and don't use any "feeling" words. Instead, evoke emotions through what the character says or does.

[11]
FEELING THE STORY: AN EXAMINATION OF *PAY IT FORWARD*

Movie to watch: *Pay It Forward*

I need several chapters to discuss the near-perfect structure of this movie. If you haven't seen it recently, I strongly encourage you to watch it now so you can better understand the concepts.

First let me say that I don't believe every story has to be heart wrenching or make the reader cry. Plenty of books are funny or heartwarming or emotional in other ways. The reason I cite this movie is because it's an extreme and perfect example of one way to evoke emotion. When I find a perfectly plotted story or movie, I'm in plot heaven, and this is one of the most beautifully plotted stories I've ever seen. This movie has every element I know and teach about, and most of all—in a really big way—it has emotional impact.

Granted, it has a sad and terrible ending, and I think the writer/director could have ended the film differently, but I use my blissful coping mechanism of making up my own alternate ending to get me past it. And the end isn't the part that makes me cry, anyway.

When I suggest you study a movie, these are the things I want you to recognize and note. I watched this movie *at least* ten times in order to dissect it this way.

The story revolves around Trevor McKinney, a responsible seventh grader who, though small in stature, makes an attempt to interact with the world. His *inciting incident* is when his teacher challenges him by planting the idea to "change the world." On his way home from school, Trevor observes people living in deplorable conditions.

Trevor is *motivated* by a father who abused his mother. He is glad his father is gone, but he believes life sucks. Metal detectors at school and his mother's alcoholism reflect his life philosophy. While Trevor's *long-term goal* is to change the world, he starts with his *short-term goal*—one person at a time—and brings home Jerry, a homeless guy. He also wants to help his mom change and to help Adam, a kid who's being bullied at school.

Trevor's *character flaws* aren't really flaws to me because he's just a kid. He's afraid to help his friend at school, so he feels cowardly. Trevor's first conflict is when he gives Jerry money for clothes to get a job, but Jerry then shoots up. Trevor crosses him off the list. Next he tries to help his friend Adam, but Adam gets beaten up by the bullies.

You have to look at all of these elements side by side to see how beautifully they intertwine with the other characters.

Arlene McKinney is Trevor's mom, a struggling change girl at a casino, a waitress at a strip club, and an alcoholic. Her *inciting incident* is when Trevor brings home Jerry. This event sets the rest of the story in motion.

One person's inciting incident doesn't always have to be the same as another's.

Arlene's *motivations* are brilliantly created for emotion and depth of characterization. She has an alcoholic mother and a history of sexual abuse and making bad choices in men—and she, too, is challenged by Trevor's teacher. Her *long-term goal* is to get clean and establish self-worth. The steps she has taken to achieve this goal involve removing her mother from their lives and joining AA. She is determined to support herself and her son, and she needs Trevor to believe in her.

Her *external* goals are to earn a living, take care of her son, and get sober. Her *internal goals* are to gain self-worth and self-respect and to be a better mother than her own mother.

Her *character flaws* are that she's straightforward and challenging but afraid to connect emotionally.

Arlene's *conflicts* are numerous: She has time constraints from working two jobs, struggles with alcohol, is confused over her ex, and fights a constant internal quandary and conflict over whether or not she's doing the right thing or being a good mother.

Eugene Simonet is Trevor's social-studies teacher. He's highly educated and uses his knowledge as a shield for safety and protection. His internal *motivations* are having an abusive father, being a burn victim, his longing for family, and major psychological scars. His *long-term goals* are to sustain the status quo that keeps his life manageable, maintain his routine, and inspire his students. This character's *backstory* is crucial to his character but isn't revealed to the viewer until it's important to the other characters and to the story—an important lesson to remember and a technique to hone. Make the reader want to know background by first making him *care*.

His father was an abuser, and when Eugene tried to protect his mother, his father set him on fire. Eugene is severely scarred. This is his *prime motivating incident*.

Mr. Simonet's *external goal* is to inspire students to see possibilities and make the world a better place. His *short-term goals* are to be safe, protect himself from emotional hurt, and to give his class an assignment filled with possibilities because one of them might actually pull it off. Later his goal is to save Trevor, who reminds him of himself. Though he craves acceptance, his *internal goal* is to be safe. He keeps his life manageable through routine and doesn't risk opening up. He hides behind words and his education—his *character flaws*. He's trapped inside himself. Caring makes him vulnerable; he's inhibited and defensive.

His *external conflict* is first Arlene's anger with him and later her attraction to him. His *internal conflict* is that caring for Trevor and his mother make him vulnerable. His fear of the unknown threatens his safety. His fear of rejection keeps him at arm's length. He can't change his own life.

In *Techniques of the Selling Writer*, Dwight V. Swain says to categorize your characters by using an adjective and noun of vocation, such as a know-it-all professor or a stage-shy actress. This also shows their built-in differences.

- He's a highly educated teacher.
- She's a struggling change girl at a casino and a waitress at a strip club.
- Arlene is straightforward and challenging.
- Eugene is inhibited and defensive.

Isn't that a perfect setup for conflict?

When Jerry and Adam fail as Trevor's projects, he tries to hook up his mother with his teacher, but at the black moment, this fails as well.

THE BLACK MOMENT

The black moment in a novel is when the worst actually happens. The character's darkest fear comes to pass. All is lost. It looks as though there's no way out of the situation. The black moment is born of the character. If your character's greatest fear is being alone, make it seem as though no one is there for him in his time of need. The person he cares about most laughs in his face or turns his back. The business he built with his last dollar to prove his worth to his father lies in ashes. This is the moment of emotional despair, turmoil, and personal crisis. It is an internal crisis, not an external event.

This film is also a primer on the use of powerful dialogue. I outline several examples below:

- Arlene and Trevor don't communicate. He pours out her liquor, and she denies she's sneaking it. So when Jerry speaks to Arlene about her son's belief that everything sucks, she asks with incredulity, "He talks to you about this?" I get choked up every time because she's trying so hard and feels so alienated from her own child. Her pain and feelings of futility and inferiority are in those simple words. Jerry replies, "We've had our discussions." At that moment, her attitude toward Jerry changes. If this homeless guy has such insight into her child, she needs to change her attitude. She invites him in for coffee.

- In a very honest and innocent way, Trevor reaches out to Eugene and asks what happened to his face. Eugene, conditioned by years of being scarred and thinking the other kids put him up to it, asks if Trevor "drew the short straw that day." Trevor turns and walks away, past the group of kids who aren't paying any attention to the situation. Eugene's face shows his surprise and regret. Someone reached out to him, and he shut him out to avoid getting hurt.

- After Arlene has to ask Eugene for help finding Trevor because she has no one else, she says to Trevor, "I have a problem." The emotion and conflict hidden in those simple words makes me cry every time. Her son hugs her. She has an addiction that has taken over her life and her self-respect, and she tells him she can conquer it if he's on her side.

- The dialogue between Arlene and Eugene when she invites him to come for dinner and he rejects her is so believable. She risked being vulnerable, so his rejection is heartbreaking. But she confronts him, and he tells her he needs his routine or he's lost. She says, "I can't reject you. You're too quick for me."

- Eugene tells Trevor he's getting an A in the class. Trevor says, "I don't care about the grade. I just wanted to see if the world would really change."

There are surprises in store for the viewer. Grace, Arlene's mother, is one of them. Her thread is woven into the overall theme. The timeline is disjointed in order to properly pace the story and introduce surprises—and it follows the reporter who is tracking the "pay it forward" story, but not in chronological order. The timeline is tough to explain until you've seen the movie.

Trevor's *fear* is that his dad will come back and that the better life he's only recently tasted will be snatched away. Of course, that is his *black moment*—his dad comes back, and Arlene thinks she should give him a chance.

I always work on *comparing and contrasting* to bring out emotion, and the comparisons in this story are huge. Visually and setting-wise, the flashy lights and big money of the casinos and hotels are a backdrop to the burning trash barrels over which the homeless warm themselves. Another beautiful contrast is Eugene's scarred, discolored skin against Arlene's perfect and lovely face when they kiss. And comparing Jon Bon Jovi in all his pretty-boy perfection to Kevin Spacey as a burn victim speaks volumes.

Eugene leaves Arlene and the ex together to go back to his safe routine, but he's been burned again—this time emotionally—and he won't risk hurt again. When the ex drinks and winds up making trouble, Arlene says to Trevor, "I think I made a mistake." Wow.

And Trevor replies, "Everyone makes mistakes."

But it's too late for her to take up with Eugene again. Trevor asks Eugene to "pay it forward" by giving Arlene another chance. "That's why this is the one," he says. "Because it's supposed to be something hard." This *powerful dialogue* wrings a reaction from the viewer. But Eugene can't let himself do that.

I explained that Trevor's *black moment* is when his dad comes back and his mom lets him stay. Eugene's black moment is the same. He took the leap and fell, and it hurt. Arlene's black moment is when she repeats the same mistake she made before, but this time she hurts them all and loses Eugene.

Each character's growth and come-to-realize moment: Trevor is quick to forgive his mom. The world's not all terrible. He learns compassion for people who are afraid to change. Eugene exposes his flaws, tells Arlene his story, admits he needs her, and in the end forgives her. Arlene faces herself, forgives her mother, and knows her son made a difference.

Arlene goes to her mother and says, "I forgive you." This is monumental. This is her act of "paying it forward." And her act of forgiveness sets the ball in motion for everything else that happens, in retrospect. We recognize how badly Arlene has messed up, yet Trevor forgives her. Though Arlene needs Eugene to forgive her and that's not forthcoming, she learns something and forgives her mom.

The reporter finds Trevor and sets up an interview. During the interview, to which Arlene and Eugene are both listening, Trevor talks about how his mom forgave his grandma, and how he got to see her for his birthday, and how hard that was for his mom. He says, "My mom was so brave." I lose it there, too—every time. Those words jog Eugene out of his safe routine and protective shell, and he goes to Arlene and asks her not to let him be one of those people that Trevor was talking about, one of those people who are too afraid to take a chance.

All of the characters in this story are wounded. The "pay it forward" backstory is woven throughout the current story. The writers tapped into the universal themes of hope for humanity, "life goes on," forgiveness, and acceptance. The key story question is "Can one person make the world a better place?" and the key phrase is "It's possible."

These are the kinds of things you should be looking for when studying the suggested books and movies and taking notes in your notebook or journal. Study each element of the story for every character, and see how they flow into each other.

EXERCISE

Watch this movie again, and experience it with the information I've pointed out to you. Focus on the powerful dialogue. Note the contrasts and comparisons.

[12]
SACRIFICE AND EVOCATIVE VS. EMOTIONAL WRITING

Movie to watch: *Slumdog Millionaire*

People read fiction and watch movies to experience thrills, anger, fear, ecstasy, tension, and love without risk to themselves. We love to jump in our seats and gasp at surprise endings and cry over romantic encounters all within the safety of our comfort zones and all while knowing we are out of harm's reach. It's the emotional impact that draws us in and keeps us coming back. We can forgive a lot if we are engaged in the story. We can overlook a slightly implausible plot, or even a wildly implausible one—has anyone seen *Transformers: Revenge of the Fallen*?—if we are rooting for the story people. We can forgive a point-of-view slip if the story has swept us along for the ride.

The emotional investment must be powerful enough to carry us from the beginning to the end, all while making us care about the outcome. A story doesn't have to be complex or heavily laden with research or setting details. It can have the most simple conflict and still hold our interest if we care. We must be able to root for the characters. I watched *Slumdog Millionaire* only once because I found the story dark and disturbing. It took me quite a while to become invested in the story, but once I did, I understood its universal appeal. The main characters are underdogs—orphans. (Remember, orphans are one of those story givens that garner universal appeal and sympathy.) We become invested in Jamal Malik's plight when everything works against him and when even his brother is a rat. His childhood friend Latika, with whom he's survived and bonded, is taken from him, and the rest of the movie focuses on his quest to find and free her.

Finding Latika is an emotional/internal goal—as well as a physical/external goal. The viewer holds his breath waiting to learn what has become of her and whether or not Jamal will be able to save her. The writers brought the characters to life with true-to-life experiences, a protagonist just defiant enough in his sweetly appealing way to amuse us, and a villain worthy of our hate. Oh, and who doesn't want to win a million dollars?

SACRIFICE IS ESSENTIAL

Your character must make a sacrifice or at the very least take a big risk. When you think back to your favorite books, the ones you've studied and the ones that are on your keeper shelf, you'll probably find that the main characters made a sacrifice for another person or a cause. *Armageddon* is a dramatic example. Harry Stamper, played by Bruce Willis, rockets off into space to drill a hole into a meteor, blow it up, and save the planet. When the remote for the nuclear weapon is damaged and must be detonated on-site, Harry volunteers to stay behind and get the job done. In *Terminator 2: Judgment Day*, the cybernetic organism T-800 lowers himself into molten metal to make sure Judgment Day never happens.

In the 1989 movie *Winter People*, starring a young Kurt Russell, Kelly McGillis, and Lloyd Bridges, Kelly's character, Collie, makes a sacrifice that tears my heart out every time I watch it. She gives her child to his grandfather in exchange for her brother's life. I still remember the first time I saw it. I was sitting on the sofa with tissues crumpled all around me when my husband came home, took one look at me, and asked, "What's wrong, honey?" I was sobbing so hard over that movie, I could barely tell him. I aspire to make people feel that deeply when I write.

Of course, not every sacrifice should involve life or children, but the sacrifice must have high stakes. A wealthy person can't "sacrifice" disposable cash or an extra pair of barbecue tongs. Think more along the lines of someone's last five dollars, the coat they worked all summer to buy, or the possession they cherish most. Remember in *Pretty Woman*, when Edward, who is afraid of heights, climbs that ladder at the end of the film to show Vivian that he loves her?

To find a meaningful sacrifice, look first at the character's goal and the conflicts she's been battling. Create something significant to your character, like her belief that violence is never the answer, and then box her in until she has no other choice but to clobber someone to save the day. That's another type of sacrifice—that character is sacrificing her values for a great cause or for love. Perhaps your character struggled through the book to set up a medical practice in a particular city, but when she falls in love and marries, she's willing to take a lesser position and live in an area where the hero can be near his family.

Rosamunde Pilcher wrote:

> What touches the writer is what will eventually get through to the reader. Understated, underplayed, under exaggerated, yet totally sincere. There has to be a rapport, a chime of instant recognition, clear as a bell. If you don't produce tears, you will at least kindle understanding, identification, and so forge a bond with the reader. And at the end of the day, perhaps this is what writing is all about.

I told you what we remember most about people is how they made us feel. What we remember most about a movie or a book is how it made us feel.

WHAT NOT TO SAY

Don't tell the reader how to feel. Don't feel it for him. Let the reader participate. Use words to draw feeling throughout your entire story and leading up to these key scenes—and then let the reader experience the impact.

Here's an excerpt from my book *Her Colorado Man*:

> Wes woke at dawn and eased out of bed without disturbing Mariah so he could wash and shave. He left for five minutes to order breakfast and have coffee sent up, and when he returned, her eyes opened.
>
> She stared at him, focusing, then blinked and looked toward the window.
>
> "Good morning," he said.
>
> Her gaze fixed on him. She looked rested, but it only took moments for that look of tortured regret to return to her eyes. "I didn't dream it."
>
> "You didn't dream it. I'll go and get a tub ready for you in the bath chamber. You'll feel better after you've bathed and washed your hair. I'll help you."
>
> She rocked her head back and forth on the pillow. "I won't feel better."
>
> "Well, you'll feel clean. And I've ordered coffee and some breakfast."
>
> "I'm not—."
>
> "Don't say it. You're going to bathe and eat and put on clean clothing. You're not doing Hildy any good by starving yourself."
>
> He heated water and returned for her, helping her out of her undergarments and into the steaming tub. He poured pitchers full over her hair until it was soaked, then lathered and massaged the wet locks and her scalp.

> "I'm not like this," she said, reaching to wipe drip-
> ping suds from her jaw. "I'm stronger than this."

When I read this section to my critique group, they noted that the last line had emotional punch. This scene takes place after Mariah has spent days at an injured person's bedside. Mariah is a strong, independent woman, and this behavior is out of character. She knows it. He knows it. But her pain is revealed through Wes's point of view.

The reader doesn't necessarily need to cry when the character does. Show your scene and your character's reactions to it from a wide-lens perspective. Let your reader interpret how she should be feeling about the character's words and reactions. Feeling words are good, but use them subtly and sparingly, and *don't* beat the reader over the head. Consider if I'd done this instead:

> Mariah was so grief-stricken and feeling so guilty that
> she couldn't eat. This burden of despair was over-
> whelming in its weight and volume. Her loss was an
> agony she couldn't bear to live with.

Argh! In this paragraph, the poor reader feels as though she's trapped in the corner at that party while an acquaintance tells her all about her ugly divorce. The information is being shoved down her throat.

> The smell of bacon and eggs made her belly rumble.
> How long had it been since she'd eaten? Picking up
> a fork, Mariah took a few bites and tasted nothing.
>
> Her hand shook as she poured coffee, and the
> liquid slopped over onto the tray. She added sugar to
> her cup and drank half.
>
> Her stomach felt full. Setting down the cup, she
> closed her eyes. Normal every day things. Eating.
> Drinking. Bathing. What did any of it matter, really?
> What difference did anything make if you couldn't pro-
> tect the people you loved?

Here, Mariah's reactions to her grief are shared in deep point of view. This time the reader is more than a spectator; she's *experiencing* the emotions that she concludes Mariah is feeling. What I didn't say was as important as what I did say.

EXERCISES

1. Brainstorm a sacrifice one or more of your main characters are going to make. It's helpful for me to make a list; try for ten or fifteen, and fill in each line with an idea. Nothing is too over-the-top when you're brainstorming. Don't quit until you find an idea you like. Consider what's most important to your character, and plan how she might give it up or change her plan to benefit one or more people. If an idea doesn't come naturally right now, set your list aside until you're further into the book.

2. Read through a few scenes in your current story. Did you say too much? Was there a way you might have presented the scene to let the reader draw their own emotional conclusion?

PART THREE
SETTING IS MORE THAN A BACKDROP

[13]
DEFINING SETTING AND OBSERVATION

Nothing compares to the experience of reading a book that makes us feel as though we are right there experiencing the story. Books that won't let us put them down until we've followed the characters to their satisfying ending are the kind we shop for, hope for, seek out. We can learn to trigger responses like those in our readers. One way to do this is through establishing an engaging and meaningful setting.

When we talk about setting, our discussion includes aspects as diverse as accents, idioms, senses, recurring characters, and weather. Period, traditions, moral beliefs, customs, and the writer's voice are all woven into the same tapestry that brings a story to life. Whether it's your hometown or outer space, the location plays as much a part in adding depth and realism as do the characters.

An author should have a solid reason for where he places characters, and a skillful author can use setting to intensify reader involvement. The chapters in this section detail methods to make readers feel as though they are in the moment.

In the next few chapters we'll go over:

- how setting affects your story
- engaging emotions and senses
- adding physical realism

- researching your setting
- weaving the elements of setting together

Writing is hard work, and there's as much a business aspect as a creative one to consider. I am always looking for ways to hone techniques that make my stories better. I'm always learning, always striving for more polish or a stronger voice—and I'm not the final authority on anything. Each of us is different in our approach to a story, and every story unfolds differently.

A story I finished recently wasn't written exactly the same way my past forty-some books were written. I found myself going back and adding threads as I came up with them, and that's an unusual thing for me. But I've learned that just because a story is unfolding in a different way doesn't mean the method is wrong. It just means this particular story developed uniquely.

I approached topics to include in this book the same way I went about coming up with my brand. I took serious stock and reviewed my strengths and what I had to offer. Over the years, readers and reviewers have often mentioned my settings and attention to detail, but I could only think of a couple of workshops I'd ever attended and only one book I'd read that addressed setting in a deep study. So I set about figuring out how I do setting, how I see it done, and how taking note of and applying techniques can help us write stories.

Decide on the story you will be working with as you go through these next chapters, get out a note card or a sticky note, and answer these three questions:

1. What is the title of your current work in progress?
2. Where is your story set?
   - place
   - year
   - season
3. Why did you select this particular place, year, and season?

Now place that note in front of you, or tape it in your binder/notebook and keep it handy.

DEFINING SETTING

Some say that plot is the backbone that holds a story together, but I define plot as a series of events that carry the story from the beginning to the end, so that analogy doesn't work for me. I'm more likely to think of conflict as the backbone of a story. Everything stems from the conflict, and conflict keeps the story hanging together from the beginning to the end. If conflict is the backbone, then setting is the nervous system. A body can't do anything if it's only a spine. It needs the nervous system to make the organs function, in addition to muscles and arteries that work in perfect unison.

When one of these elements gets out of line, the whole body is out of whack. This is how important each element of a story is and how imperative it is to create them so they work together.

If used to its fullest advantage, the setting can keep all the storylines and viewpoints tied together. It may seem obvious because of its title, but if we were to look at *Australia* as an example, we'd see a story that couldn't have been set anywhere else. No other place would have worked equally well. No other time period would have been like a heart pumping blood to the rest of the story. Every last thread of that plot is tied to the setting: the main characters' differences in culture and background, the specific breeds of cattle, cattle rustling, the plight of the Aborigines and the half-caste children, and the attack by the Japanese. The writers of the script used every available detail from that setting to their advantage. Set elsewhere, that storyline wouldn't have been nearly as effective.

What exactly is setting all about? Setting isn't just a physical backdrop, like scenery that's rolled up and down in a stage play. Let's examine the various ways setting can be employed in a story.

Setting can include historical background.

Books that include a historical setting may include true-life figures. Some may be broad and sweeping and encompass entire wars or significant periods. The scenes may take place across one or more continents or include the customs and manners of a particular society. *Downton Abbey* employs a lush, detailed setting against which the lives of both wealthy and common people take place. The Granthams' extravagant yet regulated lifestyle and their lavish home play a major supporting role in the lives of everyone they employ and much of their community. We couldn't pluck the Granthams from their setting and have the storylines work anywhere else. From the opening moments of the show, *Downton Abbey* sweeps us off into another time and place.

Setting can provide cultural attitudes.

Penelope Williamson's *The Outsider* is the story of an Amish woman whose husband is murdered. She takes in an injured man from outside their community, and he becomes her protector and eventually causes her to be shunned by her family and friends. The Amish people's beliefs, clothing, rural life, and rules and restrictions become part of the setting. Another example of a story set in an Amish community is the movie *Witness*.

Setting may also reflect the mood of a time or era. *Pearl Harbor* is a great example because it utilizes the costumes, music, and events of a country pulled together by war to create its setting.

Setting can assume the role of a character.

When it's vital and central enough to the story, setting comes to life and develops its own personality. These are settings that can be used more than once, several times in fact. The place and time can set the tone for an entire story or even a series.

In this context, setting may include stores, restaurants, and businesses, the people who work in them, the main character's friends and acquaintances, or the history of a town or building. Many writers use their same cast of characters and their same place to bring readers back to a familiar setting. And readers love this. Why?

When I mention familiar setting, I'm suggesting a place you've enjoyed in the past. Let's say it's your grandmother's home. You associate good times with this place. You connect it to sensory details like warm chocolate chip cookies or an evening of Scrabble. Whatever your strong emotional connection to a place, when it's mentioned, your brain triggers those good memories; you wish you could go back to that time. This is how a series setting hooks readers. They had a good emotional experience in that setting the last time, and they look forward to experiencing it again, visiting those people and extending the pleasurable time. Robyn Carr's Virgin River extended series is very popular for this reason. It's a small, tight community of friends who share lives, harbor secrets, and run the local businesses. I've read several other series where setting plays a vital part.

Jack Reacher is a popular recurring character in Lee Child's series. I can't forget Stephanie Plum in Janet Evanovich's series. We can't wait to see what Grandma Mazur is up to next, what will happen with Morelli and Ranger. Tess Gerritsen's Rizzoli & Isles cast of characters were so well drawn that they spawned a television series; the same goes for Kathy Reichs and her Bones series.

When you think about the books in a series that you love, or even a television series, it's the characters who keep us going back for more. If I mention *The Big Bang Theory*, what do you picture? A room in an apartment filled with nerdy things like white boards and models of molecules, *Star Trek* memorabilia, and Sheldon's spot on the leather sofa. In each of these examples, the cast of characters combined with the location becomes the setting.

Through the character's point of view, we learn how he feels about his surroundings. In the books I write, home almost always plays an important role. A recurring theme is a character longing for a home, preparing a home, retaining a home, or finding a home.

Setting characterizes. Setting is emotional. Setting is revealing. Setting creates tone and atmosphere. Setting affects character. When well done, setting convinces the reader she's in a real place—even if it's another galaxy or Middle-earth.

Setting is more than a room or a city.

Included in what is generically referred to as "setting" are languages, accents, dialects, and idioms. A period's traditions, moral beliefs, customs, and even the writer's voice are all woven into the same tapestry we call setting.

Some stories do have a setting that plays a very small part in the overall narrative. Examples include *D.O.A* and *When Harry Met Sally*—stories with plot-heavy, dialogue-heavy scenes. These stories could be plucked away from their time and place and set elsewhere, and they'd work just as well.

Stories with settings that are well developed and defined couldn't happen in any other place. *Mississippi Burning, Titanic, All the President's Men, Sex and the City,* and *Downton Abbey* are examples.

Make use of your notebook to observe and record. Once you begin noticing settings, you'll pick out elements and learn from them. Take note of the setting of each movie you watch and each book you read. Could the story have been moved elsewhere and been as effective? Notice how many elements are woven into the place and time.

Make a list of a few of your favorite movies, and ask yourself if they would have worked if the settings were switched around. Could *Dirty Dancing* have been set in Las Vegas?

Would *Pay It Forward* have worked had it been set against the backdrop of the Catskills? As you've had a chance to see by now, *Pay It Forward* is so ingeniously set that the plot just wraps around the location like a kid glove.

But here's the thing: We have the visuals of our scenes and our setting in our heads. The trick is to skillfully transfer them to the page. We don't have film like the moviemakers; we have words. The goal is to use just the right words to accomplish the task and bring the setting to life.

Selecting a setting must be done with deliberate thought and purpose because your story's believability and effectiveness will depend on your choice.

It's important to make sure your setting interests you—you're going to be spending a lot of time there.

EXERCISES

1. Get out your notebook, and keep track of setting details as you watch television shows and movies. Does the place reflect the character's personality or contrast with it? Is there an interesting group of people? How does color affect your opinion of the scenes? Are there cultural differences? Is the season important?
2. Make a list of a few of your favorite movies, and ask yourself if they would have worked if the settings were changed.
3. How is your story's setting significant to the plot or the characters?

[14]
WHAT CAN SETTING DO FOR YOUR STORY?

When choosing the setting for your story, make sure your location is a place that interests you and that you either know about or can readily find information on (unless you love the obscure and are prepared to dig!). Your story location should also be one you can make interesting to readers.

Above all, your story place must be presented from the perspective of your viewpoint characters. Your characters' reaction to or dismissal of setting will say a lot about them.

Setting reflects the people who live within its parameters. In *Sex and the City*, New York had a different effect on Carrie Bradshaw and her friends when the series started than it did in the concluding movie. But Carrie, Samantha, Miranda, and Charlotte wouldn't have lived anywhere else, evident when Carrie had an opportunity to marry and move to France but chose to stay in New York City. In the first movie, Samantha is working and living in LA and visiting NYC. When protesters throw red paint on her white fur coat, her reaction is a resounding, "I've missed New York!"

Setting, when used skillfully, can impact your story's plot, develop characters, or even reveal story theme.

1. SETTING CAN INTENSIFY READER INVOLVEMENT AND MAKE THE READER CARE.

An engaging and realistic setting is one of the most important hooks you can establish. Supplying the reader with familiar reference points *engages emotions*; sights, sounds, tastes, and feelings engage the *senses*.

The opening of your story is critical to snagging your reader's attention and engaging her emotionally. On page 1 you make a promise to the reader about the kind of story this is going to be.

On your first pages, setting must be implied rather than described. You don't have time to give details. Your goal is to involve the reader in your story so they can't lay the book down or put it back on the store shelf. In the opening scenes of my books, I use only subtle description. There's time for backstory and more description once the reader cares.

Page 4 of my book *The Bounty Hunter* contains this description:

> Ten years ago she'd begun a laundry business, tucking away her earnings while living under the protection her friend offered. Upon Antoinette's death and Lily's inheritance of the bordello, she'd used part of her savings to build and appoint the saloon.
>
> She had ordered the gigantic curving cherrywood bar all the way from Pennsylvania. The huge expanse of mirror behind it had cost fifteen hundred dollars. She was especially proud of that mirror. It reflected light and sparkling glassware and the faces of the patrons and those who worked within these walls. It spoke of Lily's enterprising success and independence. She was never ashamed to look into it and see the reflection of a hardworking woman.

The bar says much about the character. Owning it gives her satisfaction. With it she measures her success and independence, and it reminds her of her accomplishments. In the sequel to this story, which is part of the Montana Mavericks series, Lily's great-great granddaughter goes to the bar and sees the mirror and a painting by an artist who later became famous. The bar itself has significance, so there was a purpose in using it in the opening scenes.

So when you begin a scene and want to make an impression, where do you start?

SIGHT: Spatial dimension comes first, followed by light, color, and texture. Upon entering a room, we first note its size. A large room with a high ceiling feels different than a small space. Consider these examples:

> There were probably a hundred people on the dance floor, and Margaret still had room to move between the couples. Elaborate chandeliers glowed with the light of hundreds of flickering candles.

> On hands and knees, Jared peered into the darkness, damp earth under his knees, dangling roots grazing his hair. He fumbled to strike a match, and the pathetic flame reflected in two beady eyes three feet ahead.

SOUND: This includes tone, single or complex, direction and distance, and the character's interpretation of them. "The rain echoed like gunfire on the metal roof."

Sounds can set the mood, increase tension, alert the character of weather or a person's approach, or identify a location.

Picture three characters waking up in the morning. One is on a farm, one is in a big city, and one has been taken captive. Our first character is awakened by a rooster crowing. The smell of fresh coffee drifts to his room. Outside, a sheep bleats, and through the floorboards the metallic lid of a kettle clangs. Our second character is awakened by the annoying beep of his phone alarm. From beneath his window comes a metal bang and the sound of hydraulics as the trash man packs his garbage into the truck—it's Wednesday. Sleet hits the window, compelling him to bury his head under the covers. The third character wakes to the tang of salt in the air and the sound of gulls and creaking wood. His throbbing head sports a lump, the combination of stimuli telling him he's been shanghaied.

Small sounds establish reality. Now picture two people having a painful conversation that lags as they both contemplate their situation. A clock ticks in the background. In one of my stories, I used the sound of the clock in the hallway as a type of measurement for all the years that were slipping past for the heroine, who had no prospects and faced a lonely future. Floors and stairs creak, items fall, the wind blows, tree trunks groan, leaves whisper. The world is full of sounds.

From my book *Marrying the Preacher's Daughter*:

> The robber leaned down close as if he meant to take the ring from her neck. She raised her hand to her throat to prevent him from touching her. She could do this on her own.
>
> He grabbed Elisabeth's collar and yanked so hard that she jerked forward and the top button popped off.
>
> In that same second, a grim click sounded. The bandit paused dead still.
>
> Elisabeth stared into his shining dark eyes, and the moment stretched into infinity. She could hear her blood pulsing through her veins, her breath panting from between her dry lips. Was this the day she was going to die and meet her Maker?
>
> "Take your hands off the lady, or you're dead." From beside her, the stranger's low-timbered voice was calm but laced with lethal intent. The hair on Elisabeth's neck stood up.

In this scene we hear Elisabeth's collar button because of the word *pop*. We hear the grim *click* of the stranger cocking his revolver with deadly intent. Right along with Elisabeth, we feel her panic with the sound of her blood in her veins and her breath through her lips. And we hear the tone and intent in the stranger's voice when he speaks. This is not a man to mess with.

Silence adds drama, so add pauses in the action and dialogue.

SMELL: Smell is more important than we sometimes think. Our olfactory senses are linked to memories stored in our brains. To this day, when I smell watermelon I immediately envision my grandmother's backyard on a hot summer night. Use your reader's memory banks to your advantage.

If you want a pleasant reaction, tap into something familiar that will provoke it. Mention the aroma of brewing coffee or the warm, spicy smell of cinnamon. A theater smells like butter and popcorn.

If you want a negative reaction, do the same: Smoke, sweat, and rotting garbage are a few possibilities. Decaying leaves have their own unique smell, as do sewers and gas station restrooms.

If you've set a scene in an elementary classroom, you can smell it, now can't you? It smells of chalk and paste and old wood, along with the hot, dusty smell of the radiators or the heating ducts. Go further by adding another sensory element: The wood floor creaks, the metal lid of the desk squeaks, and outside children shout and laugh on the playground as a rubber ball hits the pavement. These sounds add to the sensory picture.

TASTE: It's used more rarely but can add physical realism: bitter coffee, a salty tear. Sometimes we can taste the tang of sea air or a particularly strong perfume. Earl Grey or chamomile tea is a soothing taste, while an aspirin on the tongue is unpleasant.

TOUCH: Textures and temperatures can be used often and realistically. Waves of heat undulate from the concrete in July. Cold air freezes the moisture in your nose in mid-January. Metal hand rails are smooth and cold. Have you ever gone to the movies wearing shorts and found the fabric of the seats rough on your skin?

Use all the senses and your character's viewpoint to provide insight into the character as well as the setting.

In the chapter "Plain Facts About Feelings" in *Techniques of the Selling Writer*, Swain writes:

> How do you bring a setting to life?
>
> The answer, of course, lies in the human animal himself. His world is a sensory world—a world of green grass and white houses ... purring kittens and thundering truck ... Chanel No. 5 and curling wood smoke ... fresh cold orange juice and hot crisp bacon ... silk's rich smoothness and the harsh grit of volcanic ash.
>
> So you build your story world of these same sensory impressions—the seen, the heard, the smelled, the touched, the tasted. Emphasis is on the vivid image and the impactful figure of speech.
>
> Then, with analogies, you link it all to the familiar, even if it costs you an extra word or two or three. It will be worth it. Someone who's never smelled the lunar pits now may come to realize that they have a parallel in the acrid, sulfurous, flaming smoke that belches from the shaft of an exploding mine.
>
> Finally, and perhaps the most important of all, you consider the frame of reference in which this world exists.
>
> Here is where you relate all that has gone before to your reference point, your focal character. You do this by presenting your material subjectively, as your focal character receives it.

2. SETTING CAN BUILD YOUR STORY WORLD TO SUIT THE DESIRED TONE AND IMPRESSION YOU WANT TO MAKE.

If you set a book in a desert region, the reader experiences the heat and sun.

If you set a book in damp and foggy London, the tone is completely different.

How scary would a story about a madman killing prostitutes at night be if it were set in the Mojave?

3. SETTING CAN CONVEY INTERESTING FACTS. USE JUST ENOUGH TO INTRIGUE YOUR READER, BUT NOT SO MUCH THAT SHE IS PULLED FROM THE ACTION.

In *The Lawman's Vow*, Elizabeth Lane worked this brief fact into her heroine's point of view as she's considering how dangerous the man she found in a storm might be:

> The old single-barrel shotgun lay ready on a rack
> above the cabin door. She knew how to load the shot
> and black powder and set the percussion cap.

This isn't a lot of detail—just enough to let us know the heroine is prepared and that using the gun would take some preparation.

4. SETTING CAN UNIFY ALL THE SCENES AND PLOT THREADS.

In *Titanic*, all the viewpoint characters are connected by the ocean liner and the fate we know will befall them.

5. SETTING CAN TIGHTEN SUSPENSE OR RELIEVE TENSION.

A dark gothic feel creates tension for the reader. Or the opposite can be true with a comforting and familiar setting. If a bad guy is after Jane, Jane and the reader feel "safe" when she reaches home and locks herself inside. The tension is relieved.

Isolation heightens the sense of suspense. For example, the Bates Motel in *Psycho* is located in a remote area, and few visitors ever come by. A character's fate is in question when it's doubtful there's anyone within hearing distance if he cries out and there's nowhere nearby to run if he tries to escape.

6. SETTING CAN EXPLAIN, MOTIVATE, OR CHANGE A CHARACTER.

In *Twister*, Jo Harding, played by Helen Hunt, survived a tornado as a child but witnessed her father being carried away by the storm. *Twister* is set in Oklahoma, and it couldn't have been believably set anywhere but in the Midwest.

Setting will affect your story people as well as reflect them. It will reveal things about the people who live there. Jo is motivated to chase tornados because of her backstory, which could only have happened in Tornado Alley.

Weather can convey the mood and tone of both story and character. Weather isn't just part of the scenery; it's another tool to bring your story to life and make it genuine. A bright, sunny beach has a different feel than the same stretch of sand darkened by black clouds and crashing waves. For an interesting contrast, the weather could be mild and pleasant while the character's mood is brooding and angry. Use every element of setting to your advantage.

7. SETTING CAN ESTABLISH READER EXPECTATIONS.

As soon as your reader knows where your story is set, he brings expectations. You can use stereotypes in your favor or surprise the reader and write against stereotype. Your reader needs to see your characters react to the setting, the social values, the history, and the rest of the population.

Have you ever noticed how many stories start with a character changing locations? It could be a new city, a career change, launching a business, or returning to a hometown locale. When a character changes locations, it gives the writer the opportunity to show her reaction to the new place, new people, and new situations. Change is stimulating and exciting, or it's scary and intimidating.

When we're used to a location, we tend to ignore the stimuli because we experience it every day. People in New York City aren't bothered by traffic noise outside their bedroom windows. But bring in a newcomer and she won't be able to sleep for all the racket. When I'm in the grocery store, I don't focus on the sound of the cash register beeping or the kid whining in the next aisle or even the music over the speakers. I'm focused on my shopping and the next place I have to be, or I'm thinking about making supper. But put me in the dentist's office and I hear every sound, from the phone ringing at the desk to the drill in the next room, because I'm out of my element and not pleased to be there. We tune out familiar things, but when a stimulus is new, we react.

Unfamiliar settings evoke emotions because we can all relate to the excitement or nervousness related to a new situation.

It's also possible to use a familiar setting and have the character feel differently about it. We always see shows where a home or apartment has been broken into and the person living there no longer feels safe. His perception has changed. A couple of years ago, I had knee surgery followed by physical therapy. The things I once took for granted took on new meaning. Rocks, gravel, snow, and crevices in the pavement were all threats to my safety, and I paid a lot more attention to them.

Create surroundings for the character to interpret, either positively or negatively. Setting is another tool you can use to your advantage.

EXERCISE

This assignment is intended as a prompt and may be something out of the ordinary for you—or it may fit right into your story.

Write a scene using one or more of your main characters. Take them to a cemetery. This isn't the day of the funeral; time has passed since the deceased person's death. How much time has passed is up to you. Try to fill at least two pages with a scene.

- What is the weather like? Describe it.
- What sounds can be heard?
- Watch your character, and decide whose grave that is.
- Describe the headstone or lack thereof.
- Is the grave well tended or neglected? How does the character feel about that?
- Describe your character's emotions.
- Add this thread: Your character and the dead person shared a secret. What is it?
- Use a memory.
- Use dialogue if another person is accompanying your main character.

Don't concern yourself with a hook, goal, or other elements of a scene at this point. This is an exercise in describing and using setting to reveal something about your character.

After you've written the scene, reread it and ask yourself:

- Did you learn anything about your character that you didn't know previously?
- Did you learn anything useful that you will use in your story?

[15]
USING INDIRECT DESCRIPTION

The more that is at stake for your character, the more she feels about the things that are happening around her. Along with conflict, tension, and emotion, setting must be woven into your story tapestry.

In the early years of romance, writers used a lot more description and effusive words and phrases. Today's reader is more impatient. As a generation we are used to immediate gratification. Movies are at our fingertips, and food is hot and ready at the drive-thru. Granted, books are for relaxation as well as entertainment, but as readers we want to get to the point.

Unless a book is by a favorite author and in my auto-buy list, I always read reviews before making a purchase. I once happened upon a particular book that looked pretty good to me. I liked the premise, but as I read the mediocre reviews, I found this comment: "Entirely too much narrative. I want to experience a story, not have it told to me." This reader expressed the problem he had with the book extremely well. He got bogged down with too much narrative.

Many authors and readers cut their teeth on the early books of great writers like Kathleen E. Woodiwiss. I certainly did. They were the first of their kind, innovative and exciting. Overwritten prose is evident to us now in this excerpt from *A Rose in Winter*:

> Erienne Fleming drew back from the hearth and
> slammed the poker into the stand, venting a growing

vexation with the still young day. Outside the cavorting wind gleefully whipped large, splashing raindrops and stinging shards of sleet against the leaded window-panes to mock with its carefree abandon the bondage she felt in her spirit. The rolling chaos of dark clouds churning close above the tiled roof of the mayor's cottage mirrored the mood of this trim, dark-haired young woman whose eyes flashed with a violet fire of their own as she glared down into the flames.

Today this is referred to as "purple prose." The character's surroundings get in the way of moving the story forward at a satisfying pace. Description must be chosen selectively. Be precise and use vivid words, but don't overdescribe. We want to paint word pictures, but we don't want them to get in the way. The reader wants to know what is happening next and how the character is going to handle it. Once we've set up our character's goals and given her conflict, the reader buys in for the duration and expects us to fulfill the promises we set up. He has expectations about what kind of story this is going to be and wants to move on with it. He doesn't want to get bogged down in heavy-handed descriptions.

In this next example, you will see how a modicum of description sets the scene and gives the most importance to the character's conflict and emotions.

We want to use our character's internal conflict to its best advantage. Whatever vulnerability we create—abandonment, mistrust, emotional deprivation, dependence, or social exclusion—we must use it in scene to challenge the reader to keep reading and, most importantly, to keep caring. If your character is a social outcast, then create a scene to make him feel all the worse about himself. Use a setting in which his losses are pointed out to him. In *Her Colorado Man*, my hero grew up in an orphanage, was apprenticed to a doctor, and later ran off to sail aboard a whaling ship. He panned the gold fields in the

Yukon and later delivered mail by dogsled across Alaska. The point is that he's a lonely man.

He reads letters from a small boy sent to his post-office box in Alaska and crosses the country to find the child. The heroine and her son are part of a huge, close-knit German family, and she has an important position in the family business. Everything about the setting, the location, the stability, the routine, and the familiarity is glaringly outside of his experience.

The following scene takes place on the night the hero arrives in the heroine's family home—the first time he meets her and her family. I set the scene by having him arrive during the beloved grandfather's birthday celebration, with the entire family in attendance. The abundance of people, all family, are part of the setting. At this point, nothing about the house is important to him because he's focused on the child—the whole reason he came.

> Mariah's sister, Annika, perched in the spot Mariah had vacated. "We've all been eager to meet Mariah's husband. John James has been talking about your arrival for weeks."
>
> Wes smiled politely. "Pleasure to meet you, too, ma'am."
>
> "Did you find any gold?"
>
> "A little there and there. I settled on a job that was as good as gold, and a sure thing."
>
> "As long as you survived the bears," Dutch added from across the room.
>
> "There was that," Wes answered, and several of them laughed.
>
> "Don't crowd the man," Louis said good-naturedly.
>
> Eventually, Annika got up to lead Wes through the foyer and up a wide set of curved stairs that opened into a comfortable open area with sofas, desks, and shelves full of games and books.

"This is where the youngsters who live in the big house play and do their schoolwork," she explained. "John James's room is on the left down this hall." She stopped and indicated an open door.

Wes thanked her with a nod and entered.

John James lay in a narrow bed with a thick flannel quilt folded down to the bottom. On the other side of a room, a sleepy-eyed Paul watched them from a similar bed.

Mariah, who'd been sitting beside her boy, stood and backed away from John James's side, so Wes could approach.

"Hey, big fella," Wes said to her son.

"Hey. How come you walk like that anyway?"

"Got my leg stuck in a bear trap last winter," Wes told him. "It's all but healed now."

"I'm glad you're here," John James told him, his eyes solemn.

Wes's chest got tight. "I'm glad, too."

"I dreamed about you a hundred times."

"You did?"

"Uh huh. An' you look just like I dreamed."

"Did I walk like this in your dreams?"

"Don't matter none to me."

Uncertainty overcame Wes in a torrent. This was why he was here. This boy needed a father. But how would he know what to do? How would he show John James love and teach him all he needed to know to grow up to be confident and proud? He didn't even know how to tell a child goodnight. "Sleep well," he said.

A moment of silence passed.

"Papa?"

He wouldn't feel bad. He wouldn't. "Yes?"

"Mama says I'm not too big for hugs."

Wes's throat constricted. This impressionable, fragile little person believed Wes was the father he'd been yearning for. Wes had set himself up for an unbelievably huge responsibility. It didn't matter he'd never been on either end of a night like this. It didn't matter he couldn't find words. It didn't matter where he'd come from or that he had no previous examples of fatherhood or family. All that mattered was making a difference in this child's life ... a difference for the better.

He perched on the edge of the bed. The instant he leaned forward, John James's skinny arms shot out and closed around his neck.

The little boy smelled like clean sheets and castile soap. His hair was cool and soft against Wes's cheek.

A hundred nights gazing at the aurora borealis couldn't compare to the wonder of a child in his arms.

Wes had come home.

Here I didn't let setting overshadow what was important and *what the reader was waiting for*. The emphasis was on Wes's relationship with the boy.

If you've read *Anne of Green Gables*, you have seen how young Anne reacts to her surroundings. When her uncle is driving her to her new home, everything is beautiful and exciting and larger than life to Anne. Even the ordinary becomes fairy-tale lovely in her mind. She gives groves of trees and bridges storybook names. The most simple everyday scene and task is magic to young Anne.

When I explain plot and conflict, I say, "It's not important what's happening. What's important is how your character is reacting to it." The same goes for setting. What's important is how your characters are reacting to their setting. Create setting with this in mind—or twist it to fit your purpose.

INDIRECT DESCRIPTION

Indirect description is your story person's reaction to setting stimuli. Effective description is not an unrelated list of details like beginning writers often come up with. Remember, the reactions and emotions of the observer (your character) induce a sympathetic emotion in your reader. That's your job!

Like all aspects of this craft, setting is about balance. Choosing which details to use and how to use them is up to you, and it gets easier with experience. And again, each writer is different in her approach. Some write their first drafts in a "white box" with little or no description until the bones of the scene are in place, and then they layer in the description. I have a friend who writes entire scenes with dialogue only and then goes back and fleshes out setting and movement. And keep in mind that some things simply require less explanation. I know what a bicycle or a park looks like, but I'm not familiar with the inside of a spaceship.

Always consider what it is you want to convey in a scene. Setting depicts tone and atmosphere. A heroine being chased by a bad guy won't take time to admire the china pattern in a cabinet or notice a stack of books unless the china is broken or she trips over the books. She'll be focused on a safe hiding place or the nearest exit. However, someone casually waiting in the drawing room might take note of the maker's mark on the bottom of a vase or notice when she picks up the vase that a clean circle is left in the dust on the table.

EXERCISE

Since I just told you that effective description isn't a list of details, this might sound like a contradictory exercise, but hang with me and you will see the point.

Carry your notebook or journal with you for the next few days. I understand life can be crazy busy, so I want these exercises to be useful and thought provoking without taking a lot of time. Take fifteen minutes to sit down somewhere: the middle of the mall, a park, a break room at work, or a waiting room.

- Make a list of descriptive words that represent your surroundings. Use all of your senses. Focus on something small or unusual.
- Make another list of "feeling" words that will describe your reaction to this place.
- Later, look at the most recent scene you've written. Make a list of words describing how your character feels about the city or room she is in.

Now, review the list, keeping in mind the details most important to your character.

- Find ways to use some of your descriptive words indirectly.
- Go back to the first scene of your book, and see how you can use description indirectly. Do you need to make any changes?

[16]
CREATING REALISM WITH SETTING DETAILS: DETAILS AFFECT CHARACTER

I've been asked if setting is less relevant in a contemporary novel than in a historical one. My answer is a resounding "not at all." Details in a contemporary novel must be spot-on because medical professionals, FBI agents, chefs, and lawyers are also readers, and they will spot inaccuracies. Even the casual reader will notice details that will pull them out of the story if they are "off." A contemporary novel can sometimes be even more intimidating because accuracy is imperative.

Setting creates realism for your story within the parameters of the rooms and places in which the scenes take place. Your character's surroundings should present a vivid mental image without intruding on the story. In contemporary novels the writer simply needs less description of ordinary things. We already know what most kitchens and classrooms and restaurants look like, so all we need are the unique finishing touches to complete our mental picture.

Don't give the reader a *Better Homes and Gardens* description of the heroine's apartment. Tell her instead that the week's mail is piled on the kitchen table beside a dying philodendron or that the clothes she picked up from the cleaners last week are still hanging on the treadmill in her bedroom. These are details that characterize as well as create visual images.

You will use more detail in a fantasy, science fiction, or historical novel, because the reader needs a visual picture beyond the familiar. Research is imperative, of course, but you'll never use half of the information you collect—or at least you shouldn't. You need to know every detail in order to write the story from the best perspective, but the reader simply won't be as fascinated with the exact measurements and construction of a bell tower as you are.

Like most writing techniques, a fine line exists between too much and not enough. Include just enough detail for flavor and interest but not enough to emphasize or single out a particular item above the importance it deserves. In other words, don't describe the shovel hanging on the garage wall unless someone is going to dig a grave with it later. An exception would be if your character is a neat freak and the garden tools on the garage wall are alphabetized—this would characterize.

Everyday work and commonplace actions create a real world for the reader, too. This is much easier to use in historical than in contemporary fiction. Historical descriptions add to the atmosphere and setting. For example, your historical character might start a fire with wood shavings or cornhusks in a cast-iron stove, pump well water, and lug it to the stove in a wooden bucket. This would show her lifestyle and routine and would place the reader in a rustic scene. You must convey reality differently with contemporary descriptions. You won't want to describe your modern-day character running fluoridated water from her Peerless faucet into a Pyrex bowl and nuking it in her Panasonic microwave with the digital clock for five minutes.

Most people go through a similar routine every day, and nobody wants to read about it. "She made herself some dinner," will usually suffice, but understand these are generalities. If your heroine is a gourmet cook, you may go into more detail. In the same vein, if a particular item is important to the story, you'll describe it in more detail than if it is unimportant. It's your call to define which is which.

In order to slip those reality bites in unobtrusively, you could try something like this: "The red digits on the microwave ticked backward from six minutes, but Maddie saw instead the expression on Sam's face that afternoon."

Weave ordinary details into the story in a manner that gives the reader the feel for the time and setting without saying, "This is what she's using and this is what it looks like."

Fiction has its basis in reality. People say to me, "You either do a heck of a lot of research, or you have one vivid imagination." Like most writers, both are true. The closer to actuality you make your idea, the more real it seems.

MAP IT OUT

For your own story, it might be helpful to draw a blueprint of your character's house or a map of the town so you don't make mistakes when writing about them. That way, you'll know from which direction a sound comes, whether to turn left or right, east or west, and on which side of the house the sun sets. The easiest way to do this is on graph paper, and you can draw your house or city as simply or with as much detail as you like.

My critique group created a series of books set in and around a lodge in Colorado. We made an intricate map of the area, including homes, businesses, street names, parks, and rivers so we could write the details of our setting without confusion. Our plan included a fact sheet with the history and description of each place as well as the people who worked there and their individual quirks. The timeline and the family trees were a logistics nightmare, but once finished, it became a tool we will use for every subsequent book. In our binders we also included photos of places and characters.

FINDING INSPIRATION FOR REALISTIC SETTINGS

Photographs are one of my favorite tools for visual inspiration. If I find a picture of a building or a street, I can see it in my story and therefore describe it. I have file boxes of photographs I've taken at museums and living history farms, and I love to browse through picture books. When I go to used-book sales, flea markets, and garage sales, I look for picture books of states and locations. I have a fondness for Victorian themes and have several books of Victorian homes, gardens, and floor plans.

Often in a book of photographs, descriptions are printed beside the pictures, so with the additional details you have information to describe flowers, animals, and much more. Historically accurate paper dolls, such as those published by Dover, feature clothing descriptions, including fabrics. I especially like Eyewitness Handbooks on various subjects like horses, trees, and birds because of the photos and informative descriptions. Taking time to browse through books will often unearth a treasure, such as a book on blacksmithing or Victorian dooryards. Don't forget to pick up pamphlets when you travel, and ask vacationing family and friends to watch for interesting booklets and maps. There are historical treasures to be discovered in old cookbooks and advertising catalogs, even almanacs. There are a multitude of Pinterest boards devoted to both vintage and modern clothing, rooms and houses, scenery, and accessories. While searching for inspiration, pick up a couple of books of descriptive words and phrases. *The Describer's Dictionary* by David Grambs is interesting and fun, and *Random House Word Menu* by Stephen Glazier is an incredible resource for descriptive words.

In researching the 1882 National Mining and Industrial Exposition in Denver, I was unable to find photographs of that particular year, though I did find drawings and photos of other years, which were helpful. Most of my information came from articles in a New York newspaper, so I put all the facts together, added a little fiction for flavor, and came up with the vision of the grounds and buildings.

The following scene is not quite at the halfway point of *Her Colorado Man*, and it falls at a break in the action, during a transition in location as the family moves from their brewery to Denver for the Exposition.

> The Spanglers were among the first to arrive in force to work in their building and create their displays. Of course the railroads and mining companies took over the handsome pavilion made of solid masonry and iron that covered four acres. Puffing steam engines pulled in railcars and workers unloaded their riches at all hours of the day and night.
>
> What was by all purposes a little town of western character had sprung up around the main building. The family had been fortunate to secure a location along the main concourse. Beside them a plump German man had opened a bakery and confectionery. According to information in the guide, he owned a store ten minutes away in the city.
>
> How fortunate that his offerings of ice cream, candies, cakes and other creamy sugary treats would complement the Spanglers' lager and old county dishes. Visitors could eat, drink and have dessert all in the outdoor courtyard, where they'd be shaded from the July sun by colorful canvas tarps.
>
> On the other side, according to their map, a tribe of Navajo and their agent would be displaying blankets and weaving implements.

Wes studied the map. "We're the only brewery."

Mariah grinned. "Yup."

He squinted up at the vivid sky. "Mid-July and throngs of hot, thirsty visitors."

"Now you know what all the fuss has been about." She gestured to Mr. Baur, painting the sign for his bakery. "And ice cream right next door."

Wes chuckled. "I'm wishing he was set up now."

"We can always visit his shop in town this evening."

"I like your ideas, ma'am." He winked at her.

A soft flutter, like the beating of butterfly wings, tickled her stomach. "Let's go make sure the ice machines are working before it gets any hotter today."

The details I used in these paragraphs set the scene by showing how this place and its inhabitants affected my characters and their goal to sell beer and promote their manufacturing company. The importance lies in how the setting is affecting the characters, how it compels them, how it makes them feel, and how they react to it.

EXERCISES

1. Have a character from your story visit someone's home. Give that house an attic, and take your character up there. Sit there with your character for a few minutes. Now method act in this setting and *become* your character.
    - Consider the possible sounds.
    - Look around. Is it dusty and dim, or is the area scrupulously clean and well lit?
    - Which element in the room stands out?
    - Touch surfaces.
    - Is the temperature an issue?
    - Is any object in the room unique to the space?

- Does everything look as though it belongs there, or is something out of place?
- Describe an object your character sees.
- How does he react to it?

Write this scene. It only needs to be long enough to convey your character's reaction to the attic and its contents.

2. If you used any adverbs ("-ly" words), remove them, and instead *show* the character's reaction.

3. Did you learn anything about your character or your story that you didn't know before? Is there anything from this scene you can use in your story?

[17]
RESEARCHING YOUR LOCATION

Plenty of workshops cover the topic of research, and most of those classes provide bibliographies and links to helpful sites. That kind of help is always useful, but it's not the topic we'll cover in this chapter. I have no idea what you need to know for your book, and sometimes, until you're at a specific place in your book, you don't know either. So instead, I want to share with you suggestions for making your research count and using it to trigger your imagination.

Researching your setting will provide all kinds of fodder for creativity. Most of the writers I talk to say research often gets in the way of writing because they get so carried away with it. The setting you select should give you additional ideas for scenes and conflict. Your place and time should create ways to show characterization through your character's reactions to their world.

As with any other aspect of writing effectively, setting is about the subtle use of details. By reading travel journals, diaries, costume books, biographies, and books about the era, the climate, the buildings, and the flora and fauna of your setting, you will get a grasp of what life is like for your story people. I have a beautiful book called *Cherished Objects: Living With and Collecting Victoriana* by Allison Kyle Leopold, and while reading it I thought of the perfect thread I'd been looking for in a story. Great ideas can come from research.

In order to become this person, to see and know and feel what he feels, you have to be able to place yourself in his shoes, his house, and his city.

Your setting needs to be more than a stage where you will stick your characters and watch them perform. Review your list of the three things I asked you to note on a card in chapter 13:

1. Title of your current work in progress
2. The place where and the year and season when your story takes place
3. Why you chose the place, year, and season

Your characters should have strong feelings about where they live, work, travel, and play. Why? Because emotions and reactions are why the reader cares and keeps reading. In order to use your setting to its fullest advantage, have your characters react to their surroundings. A really effective tool for you, as the character's alter ego, is to see the character's surroundings.

If you're fortunate, you can travel to the place you're writing about. But plenty of us write in historical periods or other worlds, and we need other stimuli, like pictures and maps. Digging deeper is one amazing click away with the Internet.

When I started writing, the Internet didn't exist. I spent hours at the main library. The library doesn't loan out books or periodicals donated by the historical society, so I spent ten cents a page to make copies of them so I'd have the information at my fingertips. I wrote to people, called historical societies, and labored for the information I needed.

One of the most exciting things to me now is the availability of information on the Web. I am a Google addict. I can find anything with the click of a mouse, and if I need more information, I am on at least twenty listservs made up of people from all parts of the world. Someone out there knows what I need to find out, and they are always willing to share.

ADDING CREDIBILITY

It's better to be safe than sorry. Don't make mistakes with research details. Never assume you know something if you haven't checked it out. Always acknowledge that your readers are smart. Someone who picks up your book will know about this topic or location, so get the facts right. Readers *will* let you know if you've made an error.

Also, don't assume that just because you made up a fictional town that you don't need to have factual data. Unless your story is set in a place or time period you created, you still must educate yourself on the area. The rules of credibility apply to even a completely fictional location.

I often make up my locales, but I search maps to give them names that sound realistic. I find the name of a county, creek, or river and use it for the name of a town. I plot out my location on a map, so I have a real sense of direction and place and know the geography and topography of the region.

You might be asking yourself, *I'm making this up, so why do I need all this detail?*

Because the closer you are to achieving reality in your story, the more your readers will buy into it.

We were able to buy into the genetically engineered dinosaurs in *Jurassic Park* because Michael Crichton used authentic details of scientific development to make the impossible imaginable for the duration of the story. Whenever I had a child home from school sick, we watched and enjoyed this movie. You can note that the researchers and scientists speak so knowledgably and passionately about their studies that we want to believe that dinosaurs are hidden away on some beautiful yet dangerous island.

Even when you make up something, it's important to know the real facts, because somebody out there probably knows more about your subject than you do. If you blunder and lose the reader's confidence, you've lost a reader.

Writers who create fantasy worlds advise giving the reader a reference point, something they can relate to their own world. For example, *Battlestar Galactica* is a parallel to westward expansion. *Star Trek* episodes are all character driven and parallel the times in which they were written. The common theme is always hope for mankind. In the end, if you want the reader to believe in your story world, *you* have to believe in the world you are creating.

Your characters don't exist in a vacuum; they have occupations and homes and families and histories and nationalities and all number of things necessary to make them three-dimensional and bring realism to your story. I can't tell you exactly how much you need to know; I can only make suggestions. At the very least, you need to start out with a working knowledge of your place, time, character occupations, and any additional subjects you'll be using.

Her Colorado Man is set just outside Ruby Creek, a fictional Colorado town I had used in a previous story. Colorado is a fairly common setting for me. I own picture books, reference books, and maps pertaining to Colorado, as well as books on plants and animals indigenous to the region. I chose this setting because my heroine was part of a large German family who operates a brewery, and this location could support the operation. The cold-water streams that flowed from the mountains were a perfect backdrop for a brewery.

I also had to know enough about brewing beer to decide which method the family used and why, and which year would be workable. When contemplating time period, I chose a year when bottling was first being introduced and also a year when a huge exposition was held in Denver. My actual location and the brewery are fabricated, but everything about the people, the production and operation of the brewery, and the time period are factual. Keeping facts as close to reality as possible makes the reader believe.

I also had to research extensively for my hero, who comes to Ruby Creek from Alaska, where he's been delivering mail between tent towns and postal stations. That research was probably the most difficult because most of the easily found accounts about Juneau and the Yukon pertain to the gold rush, which didn't happen until after my time period. So that part of my research required more searching. I searched for information on sled dogs, Alaskan temperatures, modes of travel, and traditional Bavarian foods.

I ended up with a binder full of facts and pictures. Sometimes I have to make an additional folder on one subject, such as liveries or beer making. In my opinion, you can never know too much about your location, your chosen topic, or the cultures of your story people.

ORGANIZING YOUR RESEARCH

If you're following the exercises I've proposed at the end of each chapter so far, you've been using your notebook and watching movies whenever you can, writing down details as you observe place, weather, and time and how they affect the characters and the conflict. You will spin your wheels searching for your notes and trying to relocate information and reference notes unless you develop a method for storing and retrieving your research. There are plenty of online storage programs and writing software that can help you organize. Find a system that works for you, and save yourself a headache later on.

In my Binder of Wonders, I separate my notes and research into sections divided by tabs. First, I create a list of "25 Things That Could Happen," which I brainstorm either at the beginning or middle of the book. I print out blank monthly calendar pages and place them after this list to keep track of passing time on these pages.

The synopsis follows, then lists of names and pictures of my story people, and then all the research I've done. (This can also be stored online, but I personally want to turn the pages and see the pictures—it's security for me. Do whatever you need to make yourself comfortable with your story and your place.)

I also hang up photographs, which I find in Google image searches. I find buildings, places, scenery, clothing, and so on all relating to my story and setting. You should also save these images in a folder on your hard drive because at some point those visuals become attachments for your art fact sheets[1] and aids for the cover artist who will design your book cover.

I usually have pictures of people or places taped beside my workspace. I look at them and orient myself to my character's home or workplace. A lot of writers use Pinterest to save story visuals. I have been surprised to see followers for the boards I've created—even for stories that aren't out yet. Pinterest has proven we are visual people. Your job is creating story pictures with words, and if photos help you do that, they belong in your toolbox.

Getting the setting right is about making it real, and if it is ever going to be real to your reader, it must be real to you first. Ask yourself these questions about the material you've collected for your current work in progress.

- Is your research convenient to access?
- Can you back up your research with proof if a copyeditor questions your facts?
- Does your research inspire you?
- Do you have a good enough feel for your place and time to release it into your writing in a natural flow as the character experiences it?

A note on this last point: Nothing is more glaring and boring than an info dump. An info dump is where a writer thinks she needs to tell the reader something and writes several descriptive paragraphs that

---

[1]Art fact sheets, or AFSs, are forms filled out for the marketing and design team. They include all the information about the characters, including descriptions, clothing, and personality, as well as suggested scenes and a short synopsis.

You will do yourself a great favor to keep track of all these elements as you're writing the book rather than waiting until the book is finished, sold, and in production several months later. You don't want to go back to refresh your memory and dig up the details. This is why creating a Pinterest board for each story is expedient. Also keep research notes, along with the places you found information, in a file. Not only does this well-organized information come in handy for your art fact sheets, but it can verify your research for a copyeditor if he questions a detail.

don't move the plot forward. It's important to sprinkle bits and pieces of your research into the narrative rather than unloading it all at once, pages and pages at a time. Always remember that, while research can be incredibly fascinating and time consuming, you will never need all the information you gathered for your story.

HOW DO YOU KNOW IF YOU'VE RESEARCHED TOO MUCH?

I have writer friends who love the research part so much that it takes on a life of its own. Once they start, they can't stop. The trouble starts when the research takes over and the writing is on the back burner.

If your study is cutting into your production, you're researching too much.

Let me emphasize this: If you get caught up in the fact-finding and aren't tallying a page count, you're doing too much research.

If you're not putting words on pages, you're avoiding writing.

Give your research a rest, and write the story. You can learn the rest of the details as you need them. I learn enough to get started, and then I begin. When I get to something I don't know, I simply Google the subject. If I'm on a roll and need to know something, I leave an asterisk and come back to it later, after the muse is burned out for the day.

Here's an example from *The Wedding Journey*, the first book I'd ever set in Ireland or on a ship. I did extensive research for this book.

> A small crowd stood at the wharf, waving scarves and hats. Maeve didn't recognize any of her countrymen, but she waved back. What a monumental moment this was. A life-changing day. To embed the scene in her memory, she took in every rich detail.
>
> "Weigh the anchor!" came a shout, and she turned to spy a bearded man she assumed was the captain. A tingle of expectancy shimmied up her spine. She held her breath.

The anchor chain had become entangled with the cables of several fishing boats, so the moment lost momentum and her nerves jumped impatiently. At last, with much squeaking and creaking and dripping seaweed, the anchor chain was reeled in. The sound of men's voices rose in a chant as the sailors unreefed the enormous topsails and the bleached canvas billowed against the vivid blue sky. The sails caught the wind and the reef glided into the bay.

Goose bumps rose along Maeve's arms, and the thrill of expectancy increased her heart rate.

In a matter of minutes, an expanse of water separated them from land, and the lush green coast with its majestic step-like cliffs came into view. She strained to see far enough to recognize the familiar outcroppings near her village, but of course the Murphy sisters had traveled a far piece to get to the ship, and it couldn't be seen from here.

The importance in this scene lies in Maeve's reaction to leaving her homeland and the excitement of a new adventure, so while I used specific details, I focused on how Maeve reacted to the stimuli. Our whole focus is to make the reader care. If the character cares about the details of the setting, the reader will care about them as well.

Don't lose yourself in research, and don't lose your reader by including too much research.

EXERCISE

Review your beginning chapter, and make sure you haven't included an info dump of setting details. It usually happens in chapter 1, along with the backstory info dump, but it can be deposited anywhere. If you have a question about whether or not something works or if you think you can't possibly tell this story without sharing certain facts, take a deep breath and ask yourself if the information is important to anyone, if it characterizes, and if it can be sprinkled rather than dumped. If you're still uncertain, ask another writer to read your pages. One head is never quite enough when I have a story problem.

Thinking about your current work in progress, ask yourself:

- Is my research easily accessible and convenient?
- Do I have enough of a working knowledge of my subject to make the narrative believable?
- Have I used too much of my research just because I knew it?
- Do I get bogged down in fact-finding?

Now look at a few paragraphs from your story where you've used your research, and ask yourself if it blends into the scene and adds realism.

[18]
WEAVING YOUR TAPESTRY

When you're creating the world of your story, you must remember that no one has ever seen this fictional setting. You have to communicate your world through the filter of your characters' senses. You must convey what they know and what they don't know. And the only tools you have to convey all of this to your reader are your words. Choose them carefully.

CONSIDERING WORD CHOICE

If you stop the story to describe something, you lose momentum and risk losing your reader's interest. All descriptions should be kept to as few words or lines as possible to keep the story moving forward.

The same rules apply when describing your settings as in writing vivid prose:

- Be as specific as possible.
- Don't generalize or use catchall phrases.
- Punch up adverbs and modifiers. "Shrill wind whistling through splintered boards" paints a vivid image with weather, sound, and decaying conditions without saying, "The old cabin was cold."
- A simile is better than an adjective: "She waddled like a duck" describes her waddling gait.

Describing *one thing* can be infinitely more effective than describing an entire room. This is a Dwight V. Swain technique I took to heart years ago and have used to my advantage at every opportunity. If I tell you that the sink is filled with food-crusted plates, crawling with cockroaches, I don't need to tell you much else about the room, do I?

When I teach about how to use point of view, I suggest to the writer that he becomes the camera. Using this camera technique also helps you to stay focused on describing setting. Let's take a closer look at the excerpt I showed you in chapter 17, with Maeve Murphy leaving her Irish homeland. As you read these paragraphs, become the camera.

> A small crowd stood at the wharf, waving scarves and hats. Maeve didn't recognize any of her countrymen, but she waved back. What a monumental moment this was. A life-changing day. To embed the scene in her memory, she took in every rich detail.
>
> "Weigh the anchor!" came a shout, and she turned to spy a bearded man she assumed was the captain. A tingle of expectancy shimmied up her spine. She held her breath.
>
> The anchor chain had become entangled with the cables of several fishing boats, so the moment lost momentum and her nerves jumped impatiently. At last, with much squeaking and creaking and dripping seaweed, the anchor chain was reeled in. The sound of men's voices rose in a chant as the sailors unreefed the enormous topsails and the bleached canvas billowed against the vivid blue sky. The sails caught the wind and the reef glided into the bay.
>
> Goose bumps rose along Maeve's arms and the thrill of expectancy increased her heart rate.

> In a matter of minutes, an expanse of water sep-
> arated them from land, and the lush green coast
> with its majestic step-like cliffs came into view. She
> strained to see far enough to recognize the famil-
> iar outcroppings near her village, but of course the
> Murphy sisters had traveled a far piece to get to the
> ship, and it couldn't be seen from here.

Everything that is going on is seen through the lens of Maeve's viewpoint. I didn't describe the clothing of the person beside her or what the ocean looked like behind her. The camera is focused on the details of this moment. First, Maeve is reacting to the people on the dock, then to the tangled chains that slow their progress, and then to the sails against the sky. It's time to sail! She has a physical reaction to the excitement—nerves, fear of the unknown, expectancy. As the ship leaves the dock, the camera takes on a wider view of the coast and the cliffs and she searches for a last glimpse of her village.

Setting is most effective when described from a character's viewpoint. Familiar or unfamiliar, what matters most is how she feels about it. Surroundings are perceived from point of view.

Select the viewpoint character that will best convey the images you want to show.

A strictly omniscient viewpoint is less effective than a focused first- or third-person point of view of a character who has a stake in the outcome of the story. To someone who's never seen an electric light, gaslight is bright. Tallow candles and kerosene lamps had a distinctive smell. What is luxury to one might be commonplace to another. Think about what's important in the particular character and society you're portraying.

Avoid using *they* because it dilutes viewpoint. *They* isn't one person with a stake in the outcome. It's two or more people. Don't ever risk letting the reader feel indifferent. The reader must care, so always choose a focal character.

COMPARE AND CONTRAST

Your character has a past, and it's one of your most effective tools. His experiences are needed as a base for his perceptions and reactions. Create experiences for him to use for comparison.

Examples include:

* new in town
* poor background
* wealthy background
* bad reputation
* dysfunctional family
* no family
* feminine
* practical
* domineering parent
* abuse
* familiar with animals
* fear of animals

The list is nearly endless.

Comparing the familiar to the unfamiliar is something we do every day without conscious thought. It's something your character must do in order to understand and become familiar with his surroundings. New experiences are exciting and hold our interest. They hold interest for your reader as well. If your character has never seen snow, have her drive through a blizzard or fall in a drift. When some of my family moved to Nebraska from Arizona, the teenagers had never before lived in an area with snow. Their reactions were priceless. In two days they spent more time playing in a foot of snow than most of the kids who grew up in the state do all winter. It was a contrast from the familiar, and it evoked strong reactions. Play up those reactions, and get the most out of your setting.

Sometimes a character is new to the setting, but sometimes your story person has lived there forever. According to their experience, your story people will notice different things. Put two men in a rustic cabin. One of them lives there, and the other was lost in the woods and has come for directions. When you write from the viewpoint of the cabin owner, he will notice everything about the new arrival. His cabin is familiar, so he wouldn't be thinking about it. But when you write from the viewpoint of the stranger, he will take notice of both the cabin and the person who lives there.

WEAVING RESEARCH INTO THE STORY

You have half a binder filled with information you gleaned about your setting or your character's occupation. How are you going to inject it into your story without being intrusive?

By using only what you need, when you need it.

Don't ever have one character tell another character something that the other character would already know! More often than not, these people share a history, like you and your best friend or closest relative. As soon as an event is mentioned, they both have the same memories, from different viewpoints.

"Make sure you fill the gas tank." That sentence is full of information if the people in the conversation have a history. A husband would never say to his wife, "Get gas before we head out. We don't want to run out like we did that day in July on our way back from Toledo, when we had to hitchhike to the nearest town and that dog chased us for half a mile." They both know this. All that's needed between them is the reference. If a reference absolutely needs explanation, make it as unobtrusive as possible.

> Jack turned to her. "Make sure you fill the gas tank."
>
> She picked up her keys. "I got gas."
>
> Jack was never going to let her forget her part in running out of gas on their return from Toledo. They'd had to hitchhike to the nearest town, and a dog had chased them half a mile. She almost smiled.

The same principle is relevant for any piece of research you want to use. "I'll just add these eggs and lemon to the mixture and then stir until it thickens" isn't natural dialogue, but beginners do it all the time to insert their research into their stories.

Your mission is to convey information to the reader or the story in a way that blends into the action. Your first pages are often the most difficult because there is so much to convey, but your most important task is gaining the reader's interest as quickly as possible. Choose carefully to paint a vivid picture, and leave out anything that can wait until later.

Here's a passage from the first few pages of *Her Colorado Man*:

> "Watch out!"
>
> Mariah Burrows ducked and ran a good six feet before turning back to look up at the crate teetering atop a stack of similar ones in the cavernous warehouse. Three agile young men scrambled from their positions on ladders and beside wagons to prevent it from falling. Two of them were her nephews, the other a distant cousin.
>
> "Don't stack these crates over twelve high," she called. "Better that we take up warehouse space than lose eighty-five dollars or someone's head. We built this whole building just for storing the lager for the Exposition, so let's use it."
>
> Her nephew Roth gave her a mock salute and jumped down from the pile of wooden crates. "Grandpa would've had our hides if we'd let that one slip."
>
> "I'd have told your mother not to serve that *apfel strudel* you're so fond of tonight."
>
> He laughed and took his cap from his rear pocket to settle it on his head. "You're a tyrannical boss, Aunt Mariah."
>
> "Mariah!" A familiar male voice echoed through the high-ceilinged building. "Mariah Burrows!"
>
> "Over here, Wilhelm," she called. Her younger brother used her full name at every opportunity. Among the hundred plus employees at the Spangler Brewery, hers was

one of the few non-Bavarian or German names, and he lived to tease her about it. "What has you out of the office this morning?" she asked.

"Grandfather wants to see you right away."

She fished for her pencil in the front pocket of the men's trousers she wore that were her everyday garb. "I'll be there as soon as I go over the inventory."

"No, right now. He says it's urgent."

She tucked her ledger under her arm and rushed to join him. "Is John James all right?"

"Your son is fine."

"Grandfather?"

"He's just anxious to have you in the office for whatever reason."

Relieved, she turned to wave at Roth. "I'll be back. Go ahead and start stamping those crates near the conveyor. Seven weeks until opening day in Denver."

Spangler Brewery spread over an acre located roughly two miles from Ruby Creek. The warehouses were situated with platforms a few scant feet from the railroad tracks, and the production buildings sat close to the coldwater streams that poured from the mountains into the wide creek for which the town was named. Three smoke stacks puffed billowy gray clouds into the bright Colorado sky. The mountains to the northeast were still capped with snow, but fireweed and forget-me-nots bloomed on the hillsides nearer. Mariah breathed in the pungent smell of fermented hops.

"I overheard Mama talking in the kitchen this morning." Wilhelm's tone was uncharacteristically solemn.

The scene moves right into a conversation between Mariah and her grandfather where he tells her he's received a letter from the faceless man they've pretended was her husband as a cover for an illegitimate child. He will be arriving in a few days. This is the point of change, the inciting incident.

The descriptive paragraph, which is only four sentences, shows the location of the brewery and is almost an omniscient viewpoint because Mariah isn't thinking about it. It's setting the scene for the reader in the most unobtrusive way possible. Descriptions like this work as long as you're not creating a pause in the action. The reader needs just enough detail to place him in the scene with the character.

POINT OF VIEW AND SETTING

Use point of view to your advantage in developing your setting. I talked quite a bit about using deep point of view, but you might have heard other terms about viewpoint. Earlier I mentioned omniscient viewpoint, which is a God-like viewpoint. This viewpoint sees everything, hears everything, knows everything. It's often used in literature, sometimes in fiction, but less in genre fiction. It's a disembodied narration.

Let's compare the different viewpoint types.

Omniscient point of view:

> A bird on its way to its nest flew overhead and dropped a stick on the ground. Paul picked up the stick and glanced around, wondering where it had come from. Mary's foot hurt, so she urged him to hurry on.

First-person point of view:

> As we climbed the hill, a bird swooped low, dropping a twig. Paul picked it up and glanced around. My foot was aching by now, so I urged him forward.

In first-person viewpoint, only one person can see, hear, feel, or react. All other characters must be shown only through what the viewpoint character sees. It's immediate and informal, but it limits the writer to one character's thoughts. It's often used for mysteries.

Third-person point of view:

> Mary trudged up the hill, her foot sending shards of pain
> with every step. A bird swooped low, dropping a twig.
> Beside her Paul picked it up and glanced around. "Let's
> go," she urged. "I don't know how long I can keep weight
> on my foot."

Third-person point of view is the most common viewpoint in popular fiction. In third person, the writer can write from the viewpoint of multiple characters, but only one at a time. Mentioning what two people are thinking at the same time is known as "head hopping."

Third person can be combined with omniscient if done skillfully. For example, many suspense stories include scenes in omniscient viewpoint in order to show something the focal character doesn't know about. Sometimes a villain's viewpoint will be omniscient or in first person while the rest of the story is in third person. It's all about knowing what you're doing and doing it with deliberation, planning, and skill. You must make your readers believe in this place and time without distracting them from the world you've created.

Setting is woven together with the nuances of viewpoint, characterization techniques, and research to create a realistic impression. And in the end, *you* have to believe in this story world you've created.

You can take your reader anywhere you want him to go, from gritty reality to far-out fantasy, as long as you make him believe.

You must make your reader feel as though the world you've created is real. How? With details so deftly woven in that the reader doesn't pause over unnecessary information.

The reader has to think, "Given these circumstances, this could happen."

TAKE ADVANTAGE OF EVERYTHING

You're in a position of power. You have complete and total command over all that takes place and the way your plot and characters are presented. Get a big head about it, and enjoy your role. You're choosing the characters and the places, so choose both to reflect what you want to convey. Use your setting for all it's worth. Your setting can bail you out when you're stuck. It can show you a new course of action. It can give you a fresh approach to a scene or chapter. And it can capture *your* imagination as well as the reader's.

EXERCISES

1. Select a location in your story, and describe how your character feels about it.
2. Describe your character's hometown from an airplane. Use a metaphor.
3. Draw a map. Using indirect description of weather, place your character on a rainy street and see how many senses you're able to have him react to: sight, sound, touch, taste, and smell. Remember, it's not a weather report; it's an experience. Weather should be part of the story and not a backdrop.
4. In chapter 13, I asked you to write three things on a note card:
   - The title, so that you'd have a specific story in mind as we went through the lessons
   - The place and year your story takes place and the season in which it happens
   - A reason why you selected the place, year, and season

   Ask yourself again now:
   - Why is your story set where you chose to set it?
   - Is it the best setting possible?

   Now think about this: Are there any further steps you can take to make your setting more crucial to the story and the characters?

PART FOUR
TENSION AND PRESSURE

[19]
CREATING TENSION IN A SCENE

Once you've created a real sense of place, it's essential to sustain the reader's attention so they *need* to know what will happen next. Make a happy ending doubtful. It's time to put all the techniques we discussed in previous chapters into play and finesse them for the most effective outcome. Use hooks to keep the reader turning pages. Use viewpoint to keep tension high by writing through the senses of your characters.

Tension is always about a questionable outcome. Deprive the character, and therefore the reader, of a satisfactory resolution until the very end. Waiting always makes something more desirable. Use elements of surprise, and keep the reader on her toes. Make every scene immediate.

CREATING TENSION IN A SCENE

Using tension in scene is imperative to keeping the reader turning pages. But pacing is also important, meaning that high tension isn't appropriate for *every* scene. You need peaks and valleys in your story. Your audience must be able to recognize the calm spots in order to recognize high intensity. Extreme pressure is not necessary in every single scene. Even action or adventure movies have occasional scenes of down time for reflection or levity or smooching. Think of the breakfast scene in *Twister*, where the entire crew eats home cooking and takes showers in between tornados. Scene and sequel are always the key to appropriate pacing.

First, make sure you've built traits into your character that will lead to trouble in important scenes. Impetuousness, independence, pride, and naiveté are all qualities that will get your character into jams. The amount of tension you can portray will depend heavily on your built-in conflict and character flaws.

Set up the tension.

Keep saying *no* to your characters. Whatever it is they want, hold it back. I don't try to fix things for them—that comes later—and most of the time I don't even worry about how I will fix a problem. Sometimes I feel as though I'm painting myself into a corner and it won't be long before I've painted over the only exit. But I don't let that stop me. I love it when I'm not sure how I'll resolve a problem. At that point I know I'm not being predictable. The best conflict is one that appears unsolvable, so heap difficult situations on your characters and make them prove their mettle. Don't make their situations easier; always make their lives harder.

Look at your character's goals, and ask yourself, "What's the worst thing that could happen?" Then take the worst thing a step further. For emotional intensity, conflict should be directly related to the character's internal goals and to his backstory. Don't rely on "incidents"—events that could happen to anyone and don't have emotional importance to this particular character—to carry scenes or conflict. However, heaping on one calamity after another can leave the reader breathless and feeling like she's watching *The Perils of Pauline*.

Here's a simplistic example: A torrential thunderstorm with hail that destroys property or crops would be devastating for anyone. But if your character's goal is to make a success of herself by growing the largest tomato for the state fair and when she was young her parents died when a storm washed a bridge, you've got the basis for a tense scene.

In the dystopian future world of *The Hunger Games* by Suzanne Collins, the government of Panem holds a yearly lottery to select two young participants from each of twelve districts to battle to the death as entertainment and retribution for rebellion. The so-called "Games" are televised, and the competitors must kill each other until only one remains. The worst thing that could happen to a young person in one of the twelve districts is to have their name drawn. For the protagonist, Katniss Everdeen, there is even something worse than that: The name of her fearful and delicate little sister Primrose is selected.

Katniss volunteers to take her place, and she and Peeta, a young man who once gave her family food to survive, must face opponents who have trained their whole lives for such a moment. Tension builds throughout the story as alliances are made, rules are arbitrarily changed, and one by one the other competitors are killed. Things just keep getting worse until it looks as though Katniss and Peeta will be forced to face off.

Katniss is an underdog character because of her family's and district's desperate situation; they live in poverty under government control and are in a constant fight for survival. In every scene of the film version the viewer roots for her to triumph. She is appealing to audiences because of her self-sacrifice and courage. Throughout the movie, each scene builds as she fights to survive. Conflict escalates until the viewer is on the edge of her seat in anticipation of the final outcome.

Romance novelist Jayne Ann Krentz said in a workshop that in pivotal scenes you should think "larger-than-life emotion and contrast." A plot is basically a series of pivotal scenes that will cause your two main characters to confront each other frequently on an intensely emotional level. Arrange these scenes in your story so that they escalate in terms of intensity.

Backstory slows things down, so plan ahead.

I explained that leaving details about the character in question until later in the story is an effective way to intrigue your readers. Don't fill in all the answers, but give them enough so they won't be frustrated. With most techniques, deciding what to use and what to omit is a balance, one that depends on your story and your characters. Backstory in a tense scene slows the pace. Save backstory for sequels, and use them only sparingly. If you need to reveal information, you can do it through a quick flash of internalization or a secondary character's dialogue. Hint at certain details to make the reader want to know more.

But keep in mind that you can't leave out a crucial piece of information and then just throw it in at the end because it needs to be told or because you've reached the end of the book. You must make the reader want to know the information by planting a seed, alluding to this mystery, and using it as a teaser. For example: "The thought of another funeral made her sweat." It's plain and simple. Someone dies, but your heroine won't go to the service. The reader now wants to know why the heroine hates funerals. The lure of the unknown draws the reader further and further into the story. Revealing too much takes away the seductive lure of discovery.

These are the first sentences of my novella *Winter of Dreams* in the *Colorado Courtship* anthology:

> Mr. Hammond's telegram had assured her, due to the mild winter, that the train would have no problem reaching Carson Springs mid-January. Violet Kristofferson unfolded his message and read it again, her gaze stumbling first over the name she'd chosen. She would have to remember. Bennett. *Violet Bennett.*

Here I've told the reader that Violet is using a name that's unfamiliar, but I don't say why.

A few pages later, the reader sees that Violet is taken aback by her new employer's occupation: undertaker.

> He'd brought her to his funeral parlor? ... She stared at the other portion of the building—right beside where she was expected to work and live and *sleep*. Were there—what did Mr. Hammond call them—lifeless clients in there now?

Violet imagines what lies behind the east wall of the foyer. She jumps when her new employer opens a door from the other side. He imagines that he sees her shudder. He has his own reasons for thinking she's repulsed, but I don't tell the reader why Violet is really afraid until much later—until it's important for her to tell him and until the reader needs to know.

The reader must know something is missing, however. You don't want to make him feel like he has had something pulled over on him once the story ends. We don't want to surprise him by revealing an important fact—we want to surprise him with the revelation he has been anticipating.

Another approach is the Hitchcock technique. Let the reader know something that none of the story people know. This is successful because it keeps the reader guessing about when the character will find out and how they will react.

In a romance, love scenes are action scenes, and if you've kept sexual tension high throughout the first chapters, the reader is eagerly awaiting this scene. If the first love scene happens at the end of the book, it's a resolution: By now the hero and heroine have realized they love each other and are consummating their relationship. All external conflicts should have been tied up by this time.

If a love scene takes place before internal conflict is settled, as a plot point or as an added dilemma, you must follow the scene with a new problem, hook, or story question that keeps the story moving. If you allow tension to drop, your story will stop moving forward.

This is a classic example: The hero and heroine share a tender love scene or a one-of-a-kind kiss. Everything seems blissful, and then one of them discovers some truth about the other that pushes them apart again. This is used often in books and movies because it works so well, but it's always fun to think up something new. Give clichés another thought when you're plotting.

Change is what keeps the reader turning pages. New challenges, new information, new twists, and added complications—all must be assured ahead of time so that your story has the potential for tension. Below, I'll be more specific regarding techniques you can use to add tension to your scenes.

Remember Rule Number One.

Again, it doesn't matter what kind of book you're writing or who your characters are—*a story is feelings*. The more that's at stake for your character, the more emotions he feels about events and situations. If you've set up your character for a big problem, you're ready to fire it at him. Internal and external conflict and character motivation must be in place to create tension. If you want a specific reaction, set up a scene or a motivation to induce it.

Use your character's internal conflict to its best advantage: abandonment, mistrust, emotional deprivation, dependence, social exclusion, or whatever vulnerability you create. You now must use those conflicts and fatal flaws in scene to challenge readers to keep reading and, most importantly, to keep them caring. If your character is a social outcast, create a scene to make him feel all the worse about himself. If your hero has been abandoned, his black moment is going to be when the heroine seemingly abandons him.

If you can feel the emotion, you can convey it.

COMBINING TECHNIQUE AND METHOD WRITING

To understand everything your character is experiencing and feeling, you can do what actors do and "method write," "technique write," or use a combination of both.

Technique writing—or acting—is drawing upon your own experience. If you've ever lost a loved one, raised a troublesome teen, or experienced suffering of another kind, you can bring back those feelings and compare them to your character's feelings.

Method writing—or method acting—is the ability to *become* the character. You don't rely on your own experience to create the emotion. Rather, you become so involved in the character's backstory and motivation that you can close your eyes and imagine how you'd feel or react in their shoes. I often spend some time just sitting with my eyes closed, imagining I'm the character, getting in touch with how

I'd feel in this situation and what I would do if I had his same life story and experiences.

You may be able to combine both techniques.

We've all read books that made us feel as though we were right there experiencing the story with the character. Those are the stories we remember and the kind we want to write. How can we create those kinds of books and scenes? By keeping it real.

You can start by *using the physical images* of the scene and by being a conduit for the emotional intensity. Close your eyes and become the character. See what the character is seeing; hear what she is hearing; smell what she is smelling. Is it morning? Perhaps bright sunlight is pouring through a streaked windowpane. Dust motes swirl in the air. The sun warms the wooden floor beneath the window, and your character can feel the warmth beneath her feet.

Is it night? The night is filled with familiar sounds with which readers will identify and that allow them to be transported. The sounds of locusts and tree frogs near a pond. A lonesome train whistle in the distance. Add images key to the scene: textures, smells, taste. It's important to give the reader reality bites to ground him in familiar things and make him remember a time or a sight or a smell and identify with it. Make him care about your character, but also make him feel the *reality* of the scene. Ground him in what you want him to see, feel, hear, experience—make him believe it's real—and then take him where you want him to go.

ADDING TENSION THROUGH WORD CHOICE

In a high-intensity scene, the character shouldn't stop to reflect on something that happened in the past. If you must refer to backstory, make it a one-line flashback, a line of remembered dialogue, or something similar. People don't pause in a crisis to analyze or reflect. They do, however, see details in oddly exaggerated focus, and those will seem larger than life. Think of slow-motion scenes in movies.

In any scene, especially a faster-paced one, avoid speech tags and use action instead:

> "I can't take this anymore!" James slammed his fist on the table.

Adverbs add spice, but use them sparingly. Using adverbs frequently is lazy writing because it tells rather than shows. James slamming his fist on the table is far more colorful than "James said angrily."

> ~~"Get out!" Mary said angrily.~~
> "Get out!" Mary grabbed the vase and hurled it at his retreating back.

> ~~"I don't want you to go," Timmy said sadly.~~
> "I don't want you to go." Enormous tears rolled down Timmy's freckled cheeks.

Use shorter sentences, shorter paragraphs, and clipped dialogue. This is not the time for descriptions or internalization or lengthy speeches. Use shorter, simpler words that don't distract the reader from the action.

Don't be wordy. Don't echo dialogue with exposition. Use specific adjectives, vivid nouns, and strong verbs.

The power is in the verb. Punch up the verbs!

> ran quickly = raced, shot, sprinted
> sat abruptly = plopped, fell
> cried openly = sobbed
> walked around carefully = skirted, hedged

Action in the verb:

> sat = slumped
> went = crawled, bolted
> looked = glared, gazed, stared

Keep the reader turning pages.

In storytelling, a hook is just what it sounds like. A hook snags readers and doesn't let them go. At the beginning of a story, the hook is the premise and setup that makes your reader buy into the premise and come along for the duration. It's the promise you make at the beginning about what kind of story this is and who and what it's going to be about. It's a question that needs to be answered, a problem that must be solved, or a teaser about what's to come.

A hook is also the unanswered question in a scene and the conflict waiting for a response. The reader turns the page because he wants to know what's going to happen next. The hook is why we don't use excessive description or annoy the reader with backstory or too many characters. We can't afford to lose the reader's interest.

Use a hook at the end of a paragraph.

Use a hook when you switch point of view.

Use a hook at the end of each scene.

And of course, use a hook at the end of each chapter.

How is this done? Say something or allude to something that makes the reader ask herself, "Why?" Make her want to see a character's reaction. Make her want to find out what happens next. Think of all those season finales you've watched on your favorite television shows. They always leave something up in the air for next time.

Keep the reader in suspense and expecting by not giving answers. Present questions, and reveal just enough information to keep the story moving forward. If you do answer a question, it should be information that only opens up a bigger question.

Don't end a scene with hope or acceptance or resolve—those are for the sequel.

Do end the scene with a story question, worry, pain, anger, or frustration—a negative reaction.

Avoid ending a scene with your character going to bed. Your reader will shut off the light and go to sleep, too.

You are in control of the story world you've created. Nothing is as rewarding as having a reader say about your book, "I couldn't put it down."

The reader must feel the story.

The more real feelings you tap into, the more the reader identifies. Tap into a comfort zone or a childhood security or insecurity. Several years back, a brand new writer in my critique group had a battered child in her story. He hid a dirty, ragged stuffed dog under his pillow. Each time the boy retrieved the dog for comfort, half the critique group fumbled for tissues. It got to the point that before she read a scene involving the kid and the dog, the writer just placed the tissue box on the table. That writer is Maureen McKade, who has published several successful books, including the novel about the battered child, *Winter Hearts*.

Ground the reader in what he knows, and then take him where you want him to go. Tap into a feeling, and the reader's memory will go along with it. I mentioned in chapter 10 the use of givens—character types, situations, or other elements that carry preconceived notions. Dogs or animals of any type, orphans, abused women, abused children, underdogs in any shape or form, stepparents, mental imbalances, grandparents, babies, strangers, money, lack of money, bitter divorces, and embarrassment all carry built-in feelings.

Familiar things stir memories—good or bad. Familiar fears, needs, or insecurities also stir feelings. Make the reader feel!

EXERCISE

Look through several books, and see how the authors handled hooks between scenes and chapters. Write down a few good ones, and think of ways for your story to keep a question in the reader's mind.

[20]
SUSTAINING TENSION

" "

Don't say it was "delightful"; make *us* say "delightful" when we've read the description. You see, all those words (*horrifying, wonderful, hideous, exquisite*) are only like saying to your readers, "Please, will you do the job for me?"

—C.S. LEWIS

Tension is achieved when the reader is placed right in the middle of the action and emotion. One of the most important tools for developing tension is showing the reader what is happening rather than telling him.

WHAT IS SHOWING? WHAT IS TELLING?

We're moving into the nuts and bolts of the writing craft, and in this chapter I'm going to show how arrangement of words makes all the difference in engaging your reader. The difference between showing and telling is the difference between drawing your reader into the scene and simply giving him a glimpse from a distance.

We could compare "telling" writing to hearing secondhand what happened at an event. We've all had an experience like that. "You had to have been there," is a phrase that means a lot is missed in the telling. Things just aren't as funny or dramatic secondhand as they are up close and personal. Hearing your friend tell you about the fight that broke out in front of a restaurant is not as vivid as being there and seeing it for yourself. A good many *Downton Abbey* fans were disappointed in season three when we were shown the events leading up to Mary and Matthew's wedding and then abruptly taken to scenes afterward. Everything else about *Downton Abbey* is so brilliant, I believe we all forgave the writers by the next installment, but would the experience have been more fulfilling had we been shown their vows? Most certainly.

We want our readers to feel as though they're right there in the scene, experiencing what the characters are experiencing. We want to close the distance and let the reader feel.

> **TELLING:** Jonathon discovered a skinny mutt by the side of the road. Taking pity on the poor creature, Jonathon fed him half of his lunch and led him home.

In those sentences I told you what happened. A skinny puppy is a *given* and pitiable. Jonathon's actions show he's compassionate, but you had to be there. In the next sentences, I will *show* you the scene.

> **SHOWING:** From the dusty scrub near the side of a road, a long-eared yellow dog wagged its tail and lowered its ears at Jonathon's approach. Kneeling, Jonathon let the dog sniff his hand. A few licks later, he felt confident enough to stroke the dog's ears and run a hand along its back. Not even a skinny dog should be all alone in the world. Under fur matted with burrs, he detected ribs in sharp relief. "You hungry, fella?"
>
> The dog gazed at him with luminous black eyes.
>
> Jonathon set down his books and opened his dented tin, offering his new friend half of his ham sandwich. His stomach would complain before the day was out, but the canine needed it more than he

did. The dog wolfed down the sandwich and sniffed the dirt for crumbs.

"Come on, boy. I won't be too late for school if I take you home first and get you some water."

The difference is that you were able to experience—*feel*—Jonathon's encounter with the hungry yellow dog. Now you *feel* the events.

TELLING: Sam is tall.
SHOWING: Sam ducked beneath the six-foot awning.

TELLING: The mosquito bite on Marsha's arm itched.
SHOWING: Marsha swatted a mosquito on her forearm and scratched at the offending red spot.

TELLING: James arrived in a bad mood.
SHOWING: James tossed his portfolio onto the desk and used his foot to kick his chair into position behind his desk. "Get me coffee."

TELLING: She felt empty inside.
SHOWING: She nodded and tried to swallow, but couldn't. Her eyes were now so dry it hurt to blink. The emptiness inside her burned and burned.
—Penelope Williamson, *The Outsider*

TELLING: He liked her laugh, but it made him nervous.
SHOWING: Although she hadn't laughed again since he'd come around the back of the barn, he kept hearing the echo of it. He felt the echo of it in the pit of his belly. It made him uneasy, like the hot Chinook wind.
—Penelope Williamson, *The Outsider*

Sometimes you need to tell events.

There are times when you will want to tell an event rather than show it in scene. For example, the reader doesn't need a laundry list of every last move your character makes from the time he gets up in the morning until the time he goes to bed at night. We don't need to know he had to stop for gas—unless he ran out. We don't care if it took her three tries to get her car parallel parked unless it characterizes her.

You need to smoothly move the story from one scene to the next or one place to another. Transitions link paragraphs and scenes and sometimes even chapters. Sometimes telling is necessary.

> After showering and donning jeans and a T-shirt, Donovan made himself coffee and carried a steaming cup to his office. He'd no more than seated himself behind his desk when his phone rang.

None of the details were important. I simply needed to get Donovan out of bed and to his office, where the important aspect of the scene could take place.

Examples of telling sentences from my novel *Land of Dreams*:

> He'd made tolerable flapjacks this morning while Hayes shaved and tended the stock. The man had eaten them without complaint.

> Zoe sat in the shade beside the wagon while he dug the last of the stones. Because of the heat, Booker forced her to drink water, but she stubbornly refused to eat. Back at the house site, he stretched a tarpaulin between two wagons for shade, and Zoe napped into the afternoon.

> Thea listened to Madeline and her stepmother coo over the progress of The Dress as they prepared themselves cups of tea and returned to the sewing room.

In each of these instances, the telling sentences are simply moving the action or character from one place in the story to another with a modicum of detail and explanation because the details aren't important. Beginning writers always include way too much detail that doesn't move the story.

A succinct passage of time or change from one scene to the next is known as a transition. Here are examples:

- An hour later, she entered the meeting hall.
- The rest of the evening passed quickly.
- By the time she arrived, her students had already chosen their seats.
- Throughout the following week he barely took time to eat or sleep.

Here are a few transitional words:

- later
- meanwhile
- following
- eventually
- now

Every scene/paragraph/sentence should either move the plot forward or characterize. If it's not a scene, it's a transition.

Please, skip the small talk.

Yes, it's how we speak naturally, but it doesn't move the plot or advance the scene in fiction. "Hello," "good morning," "how are you," "have a seat," "please pass the butter" ... as always, I'm not saying never, I'm just warning you that small talk is boring, and we can't afford to bore our readers.

Don't have one character tell something word for word that the reader has already been privy to. Summarize it: "While Rachel brought Louis up to speed on what had happened at her mother's, Monica made coffee."

Travel time doesn't need to be shown unless it's significant to the plot. We do need to get our story people from one place to the next, but this can be done with a drop-down (a couple of blank lines in the manuscript that show passage of time or a change in the point-of-view character) and then a new scene in the new location or with a brief explanation: "Later, in Kristin's car …"

It takes a lot of study and practice to create powerful sentences without much forethought. But there is much to think about when writing. Read to study and to enjoy phrases and language. Pick up a few books on sentence structure, vowel sounds, syntactic rhythms, and pacing.

▶ EXERCISES

1. Practice showing rather than telling by rewriting each of these:
   - The house was old.
   - Ralph's coffee was hot.
   - Cara was well dressed.
   - Sharon behaved secretively.

2. Read through the first three chapters of your story, looking specifically for places where you've left the outcome of the character's dilemma in question. Have you used this tool effectively? Do you need to leave a few more questions in the reader's mind?

3. Check for telling sentences that should be showing and rewrite them, bringing the scene and characters to life.

4. Check for transitions, and see if your place changes and time changes move smoothly.

5. Glance though a book, and take note of the specific ways the author showed action and kept the tension immediate. Make a list of active nouns and verbs used in those pages.

6. Make a list of weak words. Do a search and find for each one, and delete it, replace it, or rewrite the sentence without it. Once you've done this a few times, you'll catch yourself and avoid using those words entirely. Here's a brief list of words to look for: *felt, feel, saw, knew, wondered, realized, was, began, seemed, just, could, would, while, as.*

[21]
PHYSICAL RESPONSES

Body language is an effective tool to show how your story person is reacting to a particular situation or setting. The television series *Lie to Me* focuses on interpreting a person's intentions, integrity, honesty, and feelings through body language and facial expressions. Photos of real people from headline news are shown in comparison to a character under investigation. If you don't have a book on body language, pick up one or Google a few articles. Much can be conveyed through eyes, smiles, and body position, and showing a character responding to stimuli adds tension to a scene. Sexual arousal can be detected in stages, and all of these "telling" nonverbal signals are good to learn about and use in your stories.

We place our characters in a lot of situations, and they must react accordingly, depending on their personalities and the stimuli. As an example, let's place a character—let's call him Charlie—in a highly stressful situation. He witnessed a brutal murder and has been under FBI protection. He has been separated from his family for their protection, but they are being united and relocated in the Witness Protection Program. Charlie has had a couple of close calls with attempts on his life. Let's give Charlie believable reactions.

Physically, he's fatigued, and he can't sleep. He's had a headache for a week, and a doctor prescribed rest because of elevated blood pressure. Charlie's a wreck. But that's only his physical state. Mentally, he is having trouble making decisions, has lost his sense of time, and when he does sleep, he has nightmares about the killers finding his wife and children. Emotionally, Charlie's sense of helplessness increases, and the situation feels out of control. How will all of this affect his behavior? He paces his confined quarters, and even though he hasn't smoked for seven years, he now asks one of the officers to buy him cigarettes. He becomes suspicious of everyone and is easily startled.

Obviously, poor Charlie is an extreme example, and I would never suggest you use all of these reactions at the same time. But as you read through his symptoms, you felt his anxiety, didn't you? And I was only *telling* you; imagine if this was indeed a book and I had *shown* you his reactions.

Let's go to a more subtle and pleasant physical reaction. Lucas is a boy who has escaped an abusive foster home. He's been holding himself in check, afraid to expect anything good to happen to him, self-protectively buttoned up from feelings. In my book *Land of Dreams*, Lucas finds a home for the first time.

> "Morning, Lucas." A rap sounded on the door, and it took a minute for Lucas to orient himself to the room. Hayes's boots sounded on down the hallway.
>
> The smells of coffee, cinnamon and bacon drifted on the fresh morning air. The back door opened and closed, footsteps sounded on the porch, and water sloshed on the ground, followed by softly spoken words. The Angel. She could be talking to the cat, to Zoe—to anyone. She had a kind word for everyone. He heard her enter the kitchen again, and he rolled over on the crisp, cool sheets.
>
> His stomach growled, but it was a pleasant feeling of being alive, a response to the savory smells from below, not a bone-deep, gnawing hunger that never went away, not a way of life. He hadn't been bitten by a bedbug, eaten salt pork, beans or biscuits, or been clobbered black and blue for weeks. It was almost too good to be true. The church lady offered him milk and pie ev-

ery time he turned around. How long could a good thing last? He had no idea since he couldn't remember ever having had a good thing happen to him before.

Lucas's need to use the outhouse got the best of him, and he rolled from the bed. Clean dungarees, shirts and summer union suits lay stacked on a wooden chair, the only other piece of furniture in the room besides the bed. He set the underclothing aside and slid the crisp denims on.

At the returning sound of Hayes's boots in the hallway, Lucas grabbed a shirt and shoved his arms into the sleeves.

"You awake in there?"

Lucas opened the door.

"Well, look at you. You going to be able to walk in those new pants?"

Lucas showed him he could indeed walk while buttoning his shirt at the same time. "I'll pay you back," he said half under his breath.

"Not me," Hayes replied. "Miss Coulson bought those dungarees for you. Made the shirts herself. Come on," he said, turning toward the stairs. "Breakfast is on."

To hide his surprise, Lucas turned back and hastily made up his bed. The Angel had bought him new clothes. Not something outgrown and donated by a self-righteous do-gooder. Not clothing that made him wonder if the former owner had died in them. Gifts ... purchased and sewn just for him.

Beneath his new shirtfront, a peculiar feeling flitted in his chest. A warm, suffusing feeling he had no experience with, no name for. He knew shame and hatred and anger, and could easily identify hunger and disgust and desperation. But this ... this feeling was

something altogether different. The feeling frightened
him because it felt so good.

Notice how dialogue invokes emotion as well. Lucas says, "I'll pay you
back," because people don't do nice things for each other without expecting something in return. And when Booker reveals Miss Coulson made
the shirts herself, gratitude is a new experience. This boy doesn't know
how to react to kindness or how to trust. Because of his background, he
doesn't recognize that unfamiliar warm feeling in his chest, but the reader identifies love and appreciation and connects with him. The specific word choices and sentence structures showed you how to feel about
Lucas's situation.

In this scene from *Desperate Housedogs* by Sparkle Abbey, Caro,
the main character and amateur sleuth, is questioning Kendall, a dog
groomer who knew the murder victim and whom Caro believes is
hiding something. See how smoothly the author shows Kendall's surprise and fear through the main character's viewpoint in first person.

> "Jade said you wanted to speak to me."
>
> "Yes, about Kevin."
>
> "What about Kevin?" His eyes darted around the
> room as if he didn't want the others to hear.
>
> I decided to be straight up. "How did you know him?"
>
> "We were friends."
>
> "I don't think so."
>
> "What, you don't think Kevin would be a friend to
> someone like me?" He was going for outraged but it
> didn't ring true. There was a slight shake in his voice
> telling me it was something else—uncertainty, maybe
> even fear.
>
> "No, I don't think you and Kevin were friends." I
> turned to look him full in the face so I could gauge his
> reaction.
>
> He'd frozen. His dark eyes widened.

"I think you had a secret, Kendall. Something Kevin knew and no one else did. Now that Kevin is gone you think your secret is safe, but it's not."

He still had not moved.

"Maybe it's even a big enough secret that you'd kill to keep it," I added for good measure.

"No, no I would never." Kendall clamped his large hand over his mouth.

Potential sign of lying. Not "I did not," but "I would never."

"Kendall?" Jade motioned from across the room.

"I've got to get back to Cassie." Kendall stood, towering in his hoof-like shoes. "I ... ah ... I ... we should talk."

"Name the time and place." I wasn't going to get anything else out of Kendall here.

Anger affects a body in numerous ways as well. We grew up seeing red-faced cartoon characters with steam coming out of their ears, and anger can indeed be visible. Strong emotions invoke physical reactions. An angry person breathes faster, and his heart rate increases. Fast breathing and increased heart rate put pressure on arteries, causing an angry person to break out in a sweat. His face might turn red; his hands might get cold. Some people talk louder or get flustered. A lot of people clench their jaws or make fists when angry. That old adage about counting to ten is a good one because the adrenaline that makes us want to punch something is counteracted by blood surging to the frontal lobe, helping us control our reasoning. By the time we've counted to ten, the urge has subsided.

Do you see how these facts could be applied to a furious character? Do your research, and make your characters react realistically.

EXERCISE

Read through a chapter of your manuscript. How many instances did you find of a character experiencing a physical reaction? Did you show it effectively enough to make the reader identify?

PART FIVE
DIALOGUE

[22]
REVEALING CHARACTER THROUGH SPEECH

"I suppose you are Mr. Matthew Cuthbert of Green Gables?" she said in a peculiarly clear, sweet voice. "I'm very glad to see you. I was beginning to be afraid you weren't coming for me and I was imagining all the things that might have happened to prevent you. I had made up my mind that if you didn't come for me tonight I'd go down the track to that big wild cherry tree at the bend, and climb up into it to stay all night. I wouldn't be a bit afraid, and it would be lovely to sleep in a wild cherry tree all white with bloom in the moonshine, don't you think? You could imagine you were dwelling in marble halls, couldn't you? And I was quite sure you would come for me in the morning, if you didn't tonight."

Matthew had taken the scrawny little hand awkwardly in his; then and there he decided what to do. He could not tell this child with the glowing eyes that there had been a mistake; he would take her home and let Marilla do that. She couldn't be left at Bright River anyhow, no matter what mistake had been made, so all questions and explanations might as well be deferred until he was safely back at Green Gables. "I'm sorry I was late," he said shyly. "Come along. The horse is over in the yard. Give me your bag."

—**L.M. MONTGOMERY,** *ANNE OF GREEN GABLES*

Anne Shirley is engaging, refreshing, and wholly sympathetic, and I'm convinced we love her because of her effusive speech. Anne holds back nothing. Her imagination and her romanticized view of the world are charmingly sentimental. She has a flair for the dramatic, and she loves and hates with equal fervency. Anne's dialogue characterizes her as the dreamer she is. Everything is lovely to Anne, and she never hesitates to speak of her pleasure for life.

That passage was written in 1908, of course. While it remains a beloved reader favorite, it is not an example of popular fiction, nor is it written for today's readers. So while it's a shining example of characterizing dialogue, it's not as fast paced as readers may expect. However, the pilot episode of *Longmire*, a popular A&E television series based on the Walt Longmire mystery novels by best-selling author Craig Johnson, contains a perfect and concise example of characterization through action and dialogue.

We see a man in the shower. The shower is comprised of two-by-fours and PVC pipe. There are scars on the man's back. The phone rings. The machine picks up, and the recording is a woman's voice saying it's the Longmire residence.

> **VIC:** Walt? Hey. It's Vic. We've got a situation, and it's my day off.

Now out of the shower and dressed in jeans and a shirt, Walt walks past an old piano. There are beer cans everywhere. He takes time to boil water and press coffee. The kitchen is in a state of remodel.

The phone rings for the third time.

> **VIC:** Walt, it's Vic. We got a dead body.

Walt gets his jacket, settles his hat on his head, and picks up his rifle before heading out. He drives an old Bronco that says SHERIFF on the hood.

He pulls up at his destination, and Vic is waiting.

> **WALT:** Sorry I kept you waiting.
> **VIC:** No you're not.

They find the body and a rifle. Walt touches the end of the barrel and sniffs the tip of his gloved finger.

> **WALT:** Smells like oil, it's been cleaned. Smells like gunpowder, it's been fired. Smells like oil.

Next we see Walt pull up in town, and he speaks to the dead man in the back of the Bronco. Heading into the sheriff's office, he picks up a cigarette butt from the sidewalk. He gets his messages while we see him interacting with the other employees. He's going to take the body to the doc for an autopsy and plans a five-hour drive to notify the family of the deceased.

At the dead man's home, he wipes his feet before entering, asks the wife if she knows where her husband is, and then, worrying the brim of his hat, he speaks with difficulty and tells the woman her husband is dead. A tear drop hits the toe of his boot.

Walt knows what it's like to lose someone he loves.

Now he's heading back and sees an election sign along the road. His deputy, Branch, is running for sheriff against him.

> **DISPATCHER:** Walt, pick up. Vic found something.

He ignores the dispatcher. Distracted by the sign, he swerves, narrowly misses hitting a truck, and goes off the road, the Bronco skidding on its side down an embankment.

After cutting away to Vic's investigation, we next see Walt standing beside his Bronco as a tow truck rights it. A pile of beer cans is on the ground, where they fell when he got out. Talking to Vic, he plans to get help identifying the murder weapon the next day.

The next day, with his hand bandaged, Walt approaches the weapons expert at a shooting range.

> **OMAR:** What happened to your hand?

WALT: Hurt it.

That last line of dialogue says so much. Walt is buttoned up, grieving his dead wife, and skirting a drinking problem. He's tough as nails, but he's emotionally scarred. A banged-up hand is the least of his concerns. The writers took us right into his life, up close and personal, and let us see all of his flaws and scars, as well as his respect for the dead and his empathy for the widow. They showed us the way others react to him and respect him and gave us a glimpse of his past. We are hooked and want to see what happens to Walt.

Dialogue is the screwdriver in your toolbox. Like a screwdriver, which can be used to turn screws, pry lids, or stir paint, dialogue also serves many purposes and can handle many tasks. Dialogue can:

- Reveal a goal
- Reveal motivation
- Reveal inner conflict
- Show insecurities
- Reveal faith, confidence or competence, shyness, and the like
- Deliver information
- Reveal character
- Create emotion or set an emotional tone
- Escalate tension

Well-written dialogue is often more powerful than narrative. It's the life's blood of your story. Dialogue brings your characters to life. Your story people reveal their true selves when they talk, and as writers our mission is to develop these characters into believable people.

Characterizing isn't merely sticking on speech tags or using quirks and description. Characterization flows from how you develop this person and how you show him through action and speech. It's most effective when it's a natural result of your efforts. Dialogue is not real speech. It's more purposeful and compressed. We talk in broken sentences, with numerous "ums," stops and starts, and drawn-out syllables. We trail off, talk over each other, and often have mundane conversations. "Why doesn't Harry pull his car all the way forward in the garage? I can never get around it." "I know I set my phone somewhere." "I'm hungry, but I don't know what I want." See what I mean? We talk all the time, but we don't hold conversations nearly as often—and even when we do, they don't sound like the scripted conversations on our favorite television shows. One television show that comes close is *Parenthood*. Much of the dialogue is ad-libbed on set. The characters talk over each other, interrupt, and occasionally stammer or say "yeah" at the end of their sentences. Sometimes they just look at each other as if they don't know what to say. Written dialogue is more organized for ease of reading and understanding.

MOVING THE PLOT WITH CONVERSATION

Conversation is how we get to know a person, how we learn if she is someone we'd like to know better, and how we form opinions of her. What comes out of a person is motivated by what's inside her. Someone with past failures, who is reluctant to take another chance, might speak hesitantly or evasively. A man burned by a past flame may be full of bitterness and talk down to women. A person full of love often speaks with concern and gives caring advice. Someone full of hate often speaks ill of everyone and takes no pleasure in anything; he's happy being miserable.

A wise old woman may utter pearls of wisdom, while a foolish young woman's mouth may run with idle chatter or gossip. A person with low self-esteem talks about others to build himself up, may avoid conversations in areas of uncertainty, or boast about how great he is. He might never offer a suggestion for fear of having it rejected, or he may insist his ideas are the best. A confident character will show genuine appreciation for others' accomplishments and offer suggestions without insisting things be done his way. Someone who's always been appreciated and accepted is comfortable speaking her mind and knows she will be taken seriously.

Dialogue must sound like the person you've made the character out to be, with his background and education—the way a person with these same experiences would really sound. Unless you're writing something that requires more formal diction, like a period historical or an Amish story, use contractions. In popular fiction, our characters must sound like our contemporaries.

We can use dialogue in various ways. Sometimes dialogue alone is powerful. Sometimes we're so involved in a conversation that everything else fades into the background. The following scene from Mary Connealy's novella *Winter Wedding Bells* in *A Bride for All Seasons: The Mail Order Bride Collection* delivers shocking information, and the dialogue stands alone. Megan is a mail-order bride. David wrote her that he was dying, but …

> "Th … three pages. I sent three pages. One of them is missing. The second page is missing."
>
> "And what does this missing page say, pray tell?"
>
> "I'm dying. Megan. We talked about it. At lunch."
>
> "Aye, we talked about your health. You said you'd had pneumonia."
>
> "I said I had pneumonia … which I did. It weakened my lungs and heart. I have terrible chest pains. I can barely work. I can only sleep on one side because the side closest to my heart is too painful. If I cough, which I do far too much, it's agonizing. I came to Chicago to consult with a doctor. Dr. Filbert told me my heart was giving out." David paused, his eyes shifting back and forth between both of hers. "Megan, I have less than a year to live."
>
> Lightheaded, Megan turned and sat heavily on the bed beside David. "Less than a year?"
>
> "Yes, that's why I've been searching for a wife who will be good to my children. That's why no one ever responded to my second letter … except you. I was clear in that letter—"
>
> "On the page I didn't get," Megan interjected.

Nodding, David said, "Yes, that any woman I married needed to be willing, within a few months, to raise my boys alone."

"Because you'll be gone."

The lack of action and the focus on dialogue make this scene more intense.

This next scene, from *Her Mother's Killer* by Pam Crooks, shows an unexpected shift in the relationship between a woman and her bodyguard. The author blends speech with action in a way that doesn't distract from the purpose of the dialogue and feels natural.

Following her in and turning the bolt, he snapped up the light switch, then tossed both room keys on the nearest table.

Adrienne spun to face him.

"Your behavior with him was despicable," she said, her tone frosty.

"The man is an ass."

"The man is a member of the Scott's Gulf Alliance."

"So what if he is?"

"He should have been treated with the same respect you gave the Dietrichs and Ronald Kershner. You know how important this deed is to Tennessee. All it would take is for Denny Ray to make a fuss about how you treated him, and the whole deal could be off."

"That won't happen, Adrienne."

"How do you know?"

"Just call it a gut feeling."

He didn't elaborate, and she recalled how close-mouthed he could be. When he was ready to tell her more, he would.

"Why was he late for dinner?" Mick asked.

"He had a flat tire." She cocked her head. "You recognized him right away, didn't you?"

"Yes."

"How?"

"I used to live in the area. Long time ago."

"He didn't notice you at the restaurant."

"He was too busy drooling over you."

She considered him a long moment. The irritation still emanated from him. He looked grouchy. Peevish.

"I think you're jealous." The certainty of it brought an incredulous smile to her lips.

He pulled off his jacket, tossed it onto the chair. He refused to look at her. "I'm just hungry. I should have grabbed something at the restaurant."

"Oh." She'd forgotten the white sack she carried. She held it out to him. "Here you go. I bought you some supper."

He took the bag and removed the Styrofoam container from inside. He flipped the lid open, and his dark brow rose in surprise.

"I hope it's not too cold by now." She felt guilty ordering him a hamburger to go when she'd had steaming hot Cordon Bleu for dinner.

"Double patty?" he asked. His mouth, normally so hard, softened into a pleased half-smile.

Illogical pleasure swept through her. "With an extra order of bacon on top. And a side of Ranch for the fries."

"The way I like it." The huskiness of his voice skidded over her nerve endings, turning her soft inside "You haven't forgotten, have you?"

"No."

She'd tried. God alone knew how she'd tried.

Dialogue, narrative, and action are succinctly blended into one scene. A keen sense for pacing tells the author how to strike this balance. Once you gain confidence and find the rhythm of your story, this becomes second nature. If there's a lull and things need to pick up, use dialogue. Weigh the passages of narrative against dialogue, and make sure neither overwhelms.

Huge blocks of narrative are a turnoff when we encounter them; most of us skip over the text or lay aside the book. Dialogue creates visual relief with the white spaces it leaves on the page. It reads quickly, keeping the reader interested and the story moving. We need to balance dialogue with action and narrative, so we must place our characters in scenes together to keep them talking. Sequels, or scenes of reflection and contemplation, should be kept to a minimum and placed between scenes of action and conversation.

In the following excerpt from *Swept Away* by Mary Connealy, Luke is planning to get his stolen ranch back from the man who killed his father, and Ruthy isn't about to sit idly by.

> "I'm going to be right in the middle of this fight, or I'll know the reason why."
>
> Dare choked on a chunk of potato. Vince spit coffee onto the floor. Big John's Texas Ranger badge flickered and flashed until it matched the fire in his eyes.
>
> Luke slammed down his fork with a sharp clatter. "I'll give you a reason why."
>
> "I'm good with a rifle." She cut him off. "If there were plenty of us and it was a fair fight, I'd stay out. But even if you wait for John, and a lot of Greer's cowhands ride away, you're still outnumbered and Greer's got a well-defended home. It'll be hard to flush him out. I won't sit by while you all risk your lives."
>
> "It's no place for a woman." Dare tapped his fork impatiently on his plate. Even sitting the man could not be still.
>
> "I've been slapped too many times in my life to let another woman endure that if I can stop it. And I was harassed too often by that stinking pig Virgil to sit safely

at home while a woman puts up with worse than happened to me."

"Miss," Big John Conroy sounded so wise and reasonable it was all Ruthy could do not to dump his cup of coffee over his head. "This is best left to—"

"I'm going to help. You can leave me here, locked up, unarmed, but I'll get out. I'll arm myself. I'll find the fight. I'm good with a gun. I'm good in the woods. I can be of use to you. Tell them, Luke."

Luke acted as if she were pouring hot coals down his throat when she asked him to side with her. "Tell 'em what? That this is a plan hatched by a half wit?"

"Tell these men honestly how I handled myself in those woods." She turned to meet his eyes dead on. "If you won't honestly admit I'm a sight better than you, then I'm saying, out loud, to every man here, that you're a liar."

Without reading further, we know Ruthy is confident of her abilities. She's been abused at one time, and she's never going to be in that position again, nor will she stand by and let it happen to someone else. The dialogue, paired with snips of narrative, shows us her character.

INDIVIDUALIZING SPEECH

In order to give each character their own unique voice, we should be able to hear them talking in our heads. Tune out your own voice and listen. If you have a favorite actor or find one fascinating, imagine how he would say these lines. Anthony Hopkins's manner of speech is distinctive from that of Tom Hanks. We easily recognize Morgan Freeman's voice.

Individualize a character's speech in subtle ways. Everyone words things a little differently and uses different inflections. One person might speak in sentence fragments, while another drops the gs at the end of words. A professional or an English major won't sound the same as a street kid or a waitress in a seedy bar. Slang, jargon, and accents are like pepper: Use them sparingly. You want your dialogue to be easy to read and follow, not overwhelming.

For flavor, you can get away with more unusual speech with secondary characters because their dialogue doesn't dominate the story. Here's a conversation between a doctor and a young stowaway, both Irish, aboard a ship bound for America, in *The Wedding Journey*.

> "Where you be takin' us?"
>
> "To the dispensary so you can see your brother. Have you had a meal today?"
>
> "We ain't hungry."
>
> "I doubt that's true."
>
> "How do we know you won't get us down there and put us in stocks?"
>
> "No stocks aboard the ship," he replied. "Are you coming?"
>
> The boy glanced at his little brother. "Aye."
>
> They followed Flynn down the ladder and along the passageway. Flynn opened the door and stood aside for them to enter. "He's in the side room over there."
>
> The tall young man inspected his surroundings before moving to the door and peering into the other small room.
>
> "Gavin!" came Sean's gleeful shout. "Is Emmett with ye?"
>
> "Aye, he's right here, he is."
>
> The two boys crowded at Sean's side and gave him awkward hugs. Emmett, the littlest one, pulled back with tears streaking his dirty cheeks. "We was afeared you be dead."
>
> "No, the redheaded Miss Murphy saved me life for sure. Her and the doctor here. They been real good to

me, they 'ave. The doc said he'd give us jobs, so we can earn our fare."

Flynn moved to stand closer. "You two will have to take baths. And we'll find you clean clothes. Can't have the captain catch you looking like that."

"Can they sleep 'ere with me?" Sean asked.

It's important to get the syntax and patterns correct. Setting the mood for your place and time can make all the difference in hearing the characters talk. I *felt* the story so the reader could feel it.

INJECTING RESEARCH

Previously I spoke of using your research in ways that are natural to the story and don't jump out at the reader. Dialogue is a good way to divulge facts that make the story authentic.

In *Birds Do It!* by *lizzie star, Brutus, a hyacinth macaw, misbehaves whenever the hero comes near. Garr fears for the children's safety at his daughter's birthday party and calls in an avian expert.

Her brows drawn together, Birdie eased the cage door closed. "I know." Her expression brightened. "Take off your shirt."

Garr took a startled step back. Unfortunately, this was not the time for his fantasies to come true. "I beg your pardon."

"It's your shirt. Do you wear a lot of blue?"

"Yes?" His response was slow, the word drawled from his lips.

"Brutus is threatened by you. Birds have excellent color vision and strong color sensitivity. Since he's blue, when you wear a blue shirt and tower over him, he gets scared. He's not angry, he's frightened. Either take off your shirt, or get out of here."

Remember, every action/stimulus needs a reaction, and information revealed with dialogue is stimulus, so reaction is important.

LEARNING TO CREATE NATURAL DIALOGUE

As with any other skill, we improve the more we work at dialogue. In this case, practice listening. Listen to the dialogue in movies. Listen to conversations. Listening is a skill, and being a good listener means not thinking about what you might add to the conversation but drawing back and paying attention to others. Eavesdrop at restaurants and coffee shops, malls, and parties. Study the way people talk. Sometimes a person evades answering a question or answers a question with another question. Sometimes the answer doesn't even relate to the question.

A good way to introduce information is through dialogue. It should be important for one of the characters to hear the information being conveyed. Having your character talk to himself to get information across is not a good technique. Neither is telling characters things they already know:

> "I hope the insurance check we've been waiting for these last eight weeks comes today. If it doesn't we'll have to take Dad off the respirator."
>
> "Yeah, and our mom said she'd never let that happen. It wouldn't have come to this if our brother Robert would have filled out the forms on time."
>
> "But he was distraught, what with Emmy leaving him for that talk show host and all. We really can't blame him."

Not realistic, is it? In this next excerpt from Frankie Astuto's *The Spyglass Project*, the dialogue is precise and to the point. It moves the scene along quickly and reads easily and naturally.

> "You think I'm going to tell the police?" I took my jacket and settled it over her shoulders.

"You could, yes."

"I won't. I promise, I won't."

Still she hesitated.

"Why would I go through all this trouble to hide you, only to rat on you right after?" I leaned back, squatting on my heels.

Her gaze finally found mine again. She swallowed, and I knew trusting me was costing her. "All right." She drew in a breath. Let it out again. "My name is Gianna."

"Gianna." I liked her name. Italian, and it fit her. "Was the killer chasing you? Is that why you were running?"

"No." She took a moment to compose herself. "He got away."

"On foot?"

"In his automobile."

"What did he look like?"

"I don't know."

I frowned at that. "Young? Old? Short? Tall?"

"I don't know."

"You don't know what he looked like?"

"I didn't get a good look at him."

"But you witnessed the murders. You were there, in the cosmetic store with him, weren't you?"

Her eyes were moist but surprisingly steady. "I told you. I know nothing. Nothing at all. If I did, I'd tell you."

Most dialogue has an issue at stake, no matter how large or small. Sometimes it reveals life-changing information. Dialogue can convey a plot point or express the character's change of heart or growth. Other times it expresses a deeply buried emotion or insecurity. Dialogue that reveals a character's internal conflict or insecurities can be powerful.

Read through your manuscript and study one character's dialogue at a time to assure yourself each one has a distinctive voice and that you've been consistent with tags, inflections, and so on. When I was first writing, I went back through each manuscript, reading only one person's dialogue at a time to make sure I kept their speech consistent. I still do this occasionally.

Not every line your characters say should be brilliant, witty, or scintillating. You know how sometimes you feel exhausted after trying to keep up with fast-paced dialogue on a particular television show? We love the show, we laugh, and we enjoy it, but we have to listen intently so we don't miss anything. That kind of dialogue can be exhausting to read, and we don't always identify with someone who is relentlessly quick-witted. I never think of a quip until after the fact. Don't wear out your reader with over-the-top cleverness and brilliance.

HE SAID/SHE SAID

Remember when writing dialogue that men and women often think, process information, and speak differently. For most men, conversation is purposeful. It's used to either exchange information, present facts, or solve problems. Men are wired to fix things. Most women talk to build emotional connections and relationships. Compare these two conversations:

> **NATALIE:** "I had an awful day at work. Monica badgered me about the Neilson account all morning. I told her I didn't have the report back yet and I'd get to it as soon as I could, but she gave me dirty looks and I know she was talking about me to Mr. Holden."
>
> **JEANNIE:** "That hag. Who does she think she is? She needs to get over herself."
>
> **NATALIE:** "I know. And then at lunch I knocked my coffee over, and my skirt was stained the rest of the afternoon."
>
> **JEANNIE:** "I hate it when that happens. It's a great skirt. I hope the stain comes out."

Now Natalie tells her husband:

> **NATALIE:** "I had an awful day at work. Monica badgered me about the Neilson account all morning. I told her I didn't have the report back yet and I'd get to it as soon as I could, but she gave me dirty looks and I know she was talking about me to Mr. Holden."
>
> **JASON:** "Go to Holden and tell him the situation. He can set Monica straight."
>
> **NATALIE:** "I can't do that. I don't want her to know she's getting to me. And I don't want him to think I'm not capable of handling it myself."
>
> **JASON:** "Are you?"
>
> **NATALIE:** "Of course I am. And then at lunch I knocked my coffee over, and my skirt was stained the rest of the afternoon."
>
> **JASON:** "You should take that cup with the lid on it so that doesn't happen."

Jason's response was far less satisfying to Natalie than Jeannie's. Jason wanted to make everything better and fix Natalie's problems, while Natalie just wanted someone to hear her out and sympathize.

Most men and women communicate differently in other ways, too:

- Men make less direct eye contact because it can be interpreted as challenging, straightforward, or aggressive. Eye contact maintains dominance. Women look into each other's eyes and faces as they speak but glance away occasionally.
- Men say things directly. They don't hedge around a question or a fact. They don't often say, "We should probably …" or, "It seems as though …" When women bring up a suggestion, they don't want to seem bossy, so they say, "Maybe it would be a good idea if …" or "We could try …"

* Men have a greater tendency to talk about accomplishments. Many women downplay their accomplishments because they don't want to come across as conceited.
* Men ask a question because they want an answer: "Who won the game last night?" Women ask questions to start a conversation: "Where did you get that bracelet?"

These are generalities, of course, and you must always keep in mind the background and personality of the person for whom you're writing dialogue. Tailor-made dialogue suits the character and makes her unique. There are always exceptions to the rules and characters who don't conform to generalities. You might have a female lead in a male-dominated environment whose speech will be more in line with others around her. As always, use all the backstory events that have shaped her life to make her dimensional. As in life, people who are frequently around each other have more intimate relationships and more intimate conversations.

Confident people take their time before speaking. Dominant people control the conversation with their stillness. A submissive person speaks nervously and fidgets.

It's imperative to make it perfectly clear who is speaking at all times. The reader should never have to go back and look from line to line to see who said what. Sometimes the manner of speech is enough. Other times action leads into the dialogue:

> Missy set her cup down hard enough to slosh coffee onto the table. "He did *what*?"

I recommend using action to identify the speaker whenever possible. It keeps the scene running smoothly. Of course, you can't have every line of dialogue identified by action because if you did, your story people would be popping all over the place.

Sometimes internal narrative can identify the speaker:

> She wasn't going to get away with this. "Stop right there."

WHEN IN DOUBT, USE *SAID*

A dialogue tag is the "he said" or "she said" that identifies the speaker. It's sometimes called an attribution. The best dialogue needs very few tags. Notice the lack of tags in this scene between two men in a small-town sheriff's office, from my novel *Hometown Sheriff*:

> Nick stared at the stack of work on his desk. On top was a folder that he'd been opening, then closing and ignoring, for most of the week. Finally, he took out all the data and reports and looked them over again.
>
> "I got findings back on those bullet casings," he told Bryce.
>
> "What'd they say?"
>
> "Pretty vague. Shells from a .22, as we knew. I'm going to visit Mrs. Pascal today."
>
> "Old lady Pascal?"
>
> Nick nodded. "I want you to come with me."
>
> Bryce's grin inched up one side of his mouth. "You need backup, boss?"
>
> "I need a diversion."
>
> "You think the old gal has a .22 she's firing?"
>
> "Those casings were under her porch railing, so it's likely. Her husband could have had an army issue weapon, or something for target practice. Even a squirrel gun."
>
> "What do you want me to do?"
>
> "I don't know. Have her show you her roses or something. Give me some time to look around her house."
>
> "You don't have a search warrant."
>
> "Actually, I do. But I don't want to frighten her by going in like a SWAT team."

My critique group had a special stamp made for me. It says, "NOT A DIALOGUE TAG." It was intended as a joke, but I've used it often since

I received it. I am picky about attributions. There is always a comma before a dialogue tag. If there's a period, it's not a dialogue tag.

> **PROPER DIALOGUE TAG:** "He looks silly in that hat," Bernard said.
>
> **NOT A DIALOGUE TAG:** "He looks silly in that hat," Bernard growled.
>
> **NOT A DIALOGUE TAG, BUT CORRECT USAGE:** "He looks silly in that hat." Bernard growled.

Yes, variety keeps our writing interesting, but one exception I make regards dialogue tags. You will see *said* synonyms used frequently in some writers' work, and they aren't a bad thing when sprinkled sparingly throughout a book. But overuse is glaring. Some tags you see imply an impossible action and are not really *said* synonyms. *Giggled* is not a dialogue tag. If you want to say she laughed, make it a sentence, not a tag. Or say, "… she said with a laugh." That's a tag. Unobtrusive tags can be slipped in without giving the reader pause. Words like *added, agreed, continued*, and *suggested* aren't invasive.

Other words used as dialogue tags scream for us to stop and look at them. *Ejaculated* (really?), *thundered, howled, spewed, croaked, jeered, wheezed*, and *choked* are glaringly obvious. We don't want the reader to stop and look at the tag. We want them to hear the dialogue.

Said is always the best choice. *Said* is like a ketchup stain on rose-patterned wallpaper: It's there, but nobody's paying any attention to it. That's how we want our dialogue tags to blend in.

FEELING ➡ ACTION ➡ SPEECH

In order to keep dialogue seamless, keep the reading experience as smooth as possible for the reader. We must stay true to the pattern of motivation ➡ reaction/feeling ➡ speech. Motivation must *always* come before reaction. Have you ever been passing a car in a parking lot as a driver remotely locks the doors, causing the horn to blare? Bet you jumped. The horn led to the jump.

A startled person doesn't decide to jump; he simply jumps. However, speech demands conscious thought.

> **MOTIVATION:** George produced a package wrapped with red paper and a bow.
> **FEELING:** Harriet focused on the gift. It wasn't a special occasion or anything.
> **ACTION:** She accepted the gift and met his eyes.
> **SPEECH:** "What's this for?"
>
> **MOTIVATION:** "I saw it, and I thought of you."
> **FEELING:** A warm glow of appreciation suffused her.
> **ACTION:** She smiled.
> **SPEECH:** "Thank you."

Over and over and over.

1. Feeling
2. Action
3. Speech

You don't always have to use all three, but even if you use two, they should be in order.

> A shrill whistle pierced the afternoon stillness. Amy glanced at her watch. "I guess it's time for lunch."

Don't describe the way something is said before it is said:

> He spoke with deliberate meaning as he said, "I don't want you here tonight.

The *as* above is the clue that the Motivation à Reaction pattern is off. Instead, write:

> "I don't want you here tonight." His meaning was clear.

1. Go through your manuscript, reading one character's dialogue and viewpoint at a time. Check that you've made each person think and speak differently.

2. Print out a chapter, and look at the visual appeal of the blank spaces created by sections of dialogue. Do you need to add more conversation?

3. Do the men think and sound like typical men? Do the women think and sound like typical women?

4. Have you used distracting speech tags? Have you used speech tags correctly?

5. Looking at one scene at a time, can you state the purpose of the dialogue? Does it move the plot, reveal information, characterize, and set an emotional tone?

6. Place two of your characters in a scene, and write dialogue that shows one of them having an internal struggle and then revealing something he's kept buried until now. What is at stake? What is the reaction of both characters to this new development?

[23]
EXPRESSING EMOTION BY OMISSION

Previously I mentioned that it's more effective not to tell the reader how to feel with oppressive "feeling" words in narrative. The same goes for dialogue. Often, what is left unspoken says more than words.

This story starts out with an accident that leaves the heroine trapped in her car on the side of a cliff. See how Victoria Bylin, author of *From Nick With Love*, used dialogue to show her fear.

> "I-I'm afraid to m-m-move."
>
> "I can see why." If he stayed calm, so would she. "We have to get you out of there."
>
> She shook her head. "If I move, the car will f-f-fall."
>
> "We'll work fast."
>
> Pressed against the seat, she had one foot on the brake and was pushing as if her strength alone could hold the car in place. It couldn't. Neither could his. God alone had that power. Nick hoped He planned to be merciful today, because he couldn't bear for Leona to lose Kate.
>
> Her pale eyes flared into black disks. "Did you call 911?"
>
> "They're on their way."
>
> "How long?"
>
> "Ten minutes. We can't wait." His gaze shifted to the bottom of the canyon. A few boulders jutted from the

mountain, but most of the remaining drop—two hundred feet at least—resembled an expert level ski slope. Nothing at all blocked the fall.

If Kate kept panting, she'd hyperventilate. And if she thought too much, she'd be paralyzed with fear. He inched closer, braced against the slope and kept his voice casual. "I'm going to pull you out of there."

He reached through the window, popped the door lock and prayed God would keep the BMW steady for the two seconds he needed to open the door and pull her free. He hated to break her gaze, but they had one shot to get the angles right. He stepped back, gripped the door handle and prepared to grab her. The next step would be difficult. "You have to undo the seatbelt."

"I-I c-can't move."

"Yes, you can."

"B-b-but—"

"Trust me, Kate. I won't let you fall."

"You know my name—how—"

"Later," he said firmly. "We'll do it on the count of three."

She inched her hand to the seatbelt release button, closed her eyes and pushed. The belt rolled smoothly into place. In the distance, a siren wailed. "Wait!" she cried. "They're coming!"

A root pushed through the crumbling earth. "There's no time."

"But—"

He gripped her wrist through the window. "One—"

"No!"

"Two."

Her fingers dug into his leather sleeve. Before he said "three," a branch snapped and the BMW started to roll.

In the above dialogue, short sentences with punch, combined with the other character's viewpoint observations, show Kate's fear. The author doesn't weigh us down by telling us how afraid she is.

In this next scene, the female character of my novel *Hometown Sheriff* has hidden humiliating financial problems until now. Look for attributions below:

"Are you selling the house because you need money?"

"Why do you think that?"

"I'm not Magnum, but I did get an obvious clue or two." Nick brushed her hair from her shoulder. "You're selling your car. Now you're selling the house. Apparently, you sold your business."

Ryanne's entire body burned with humiliation. She took a few steps back, creating more distance between them.

"I thought maybe, if you'd let me, I could help you out. I have a little money."

Her worst nightmare was unfolding—worse than losing the business and her self-respect, worse than losing Nick as a friend. Now he'd know her secret shame. Her blood pounded in her ears. "Even if that was true, why would you want to help me?"

"Because I care," he answered simply.

"Even if it was true and you had enough money to give me—it could be a huge amount, you don't know— it could be possible that I couldn't begin to pay it back for a good long time. But trust me, Nick, you don't know what you're offering."

"So it's a lot of money?"

She hadn't denied it. She'd walked right into his questions unprepared and hadn't had a response to satisfy his curiosity. "Okay, I owe a lot of money. There."

"Let me help you."

"We're talking tens of thousands here, not a few hundred in a savings account."

Something flared in his eyes. "Okay."

"Close to a hundred grand." That ought to send him running.

"Okay. It's yours."

She stared at him. "You have a hundred grand."

"Yes."

"And you'd give it to me."

"Sure."

"Why?"

"It's only money. If I can't use it to help the people I—I care about, what good is it?"

"Where did you get a hundred grand to throw away?" she asked, completely baffled.

His tightened jaw revealed his irritation with the question. He got up and moved to the edge of the sofa. "I've done pretty well with my *little hobby*."

"Fixing cars?"

"Restoring classics. Making customized parts for collectors."

"You're serious?"

He nodded. "You know those magazines you saw in my room?" At her nod, he went on. "If you'd looked closely, you'd have seen my cars and parts featured. I have a Website I sell from, too."

Information was revealed about both characters in that dialogue exchange, using only one *answered* and one *asked*. The dialogue carried the scene without distracting tags. There is sarcasm in the words "little hobby," when Nick modestly says he's done okay at his side job. To Ryanne he never seemed ambitious, and her disbelief at his success is insulting.

THE WORDS BEHIND THE WORDS

The alluded-to meaning behind words is known as subtext.

In this scene from *Hannah's Beau* by Renee Ryan, the author never says it outright but implies when describing this home that the owner refuses to accept her age.

> If houses had gender, this one was surely female. Elegant, whimsical, the two-story building was made of rose-colored stone. The bold lines of the roof and sharp angles were softened by rounded windows and sweeping vines. On closer inspection the house looked a bit neglected; the twisting wisteria covered a few sags and wrinkles that made the building look like a woman refusing to accept her age.

In the following scene from Winnie Griggs's *Something More*, Elthia has arrived at her destination via stagecoach and is about to disembark.

> She picked up the basket that served as Poppy's carrier, tightened her hold on her parasol, and shifted forward. Moving to the door as if it were heaven's gate itself, she barely avoided a tumble when the coach lurched and then stilled again.
>
> "Ooof!"
>
> She turned to apologize to the passenger she'd inadvertently jabbed with her parasol. "Mr. Jenkins, I'm so—"
>
> "Watch out!"
>
> Elthia pivoted, this time carefully pointing her parasol toward the floor. "Oh dear, Miss Simms, I didn't mean—"
>
> The matronly woman gave her a tight smile as she straightened her tipsily-angled hat. "That's all right, dear. This is your stop, isn't it? You just go on now. Don't want to keep whoever's meeting you waiting."
>
> "But—"

"No, really, just go on."

Elthia looked around. Several other passengers were enthusiastically nodding agreement. Really, this was just the nicest group of people. Especially considering the fuss Poppy had made with his yipping eagerness to get to know the other passengers this past hour.

She gave them all a big smile, then stepped through the coach door, ready to begin her new life.

As Griggs writes, "Elthia thinks everyone is being friendly and is clueless to the undercurrents. By observing the words and actions of the other passengers, the reader recognizes they are glad to see the last of her and her troublesome dog."

In *Star Wars*, Princess Leia never says the words, "My people mean everything to me," but her actions show it in her every decision. You don't have to tell someone the person beside you is your best friend if your speech and body language show it.

In the following excerpt from *Stealing the Preacher* by Karen Witemeyer, the lawman wants the preacher to file charges against the man who abducted him from a train. The parson wants to extend mercy for the sake of the ex-outlaw's daughter.

"I got a sermon idea for you," the lawman said, his dark eyes narrowed slightly. "Proverbs 21:3. 'To do justice and judgment is more acceptable to the Lord than sacrifice.' Might want to spend some time ponderin' that one."

"I've been leaning more toward Proverbs 16:6," Crockett answered without so much as a blink. "By mercy and truth iniquity is purged: and by the fear of the Lord men depart from evil.'" Before the lawman could respond, Crockett took her arm and led her out of the house.

As he steered her to where their wagon waited, Joanna hid her concern over the odd conversation.

She doubted either man had actually been talking about sermons. They'd definitely been tugging on opposite ends of a doctrinal rope, though, and she could only deduce that her father was somehow at the center of it.

The above examples are all deliberate subtext. But sometimes subtext comes through on its own because the writer's principles or hang-ups are bleeding through. I've known a couple of women who were excellent writers, but their negative attitudes and feelings toward men escaped between the lines of their stories.

Readers often feel they know an author because they've read their books. To a degree, this is often true. We write from our individual worldviews, using the beliefs and understanding we have of the world and others. Readers are looking to enjoy stories—even those with verbal sparring matches, family feuds, and battles. The difference in the words you choose makes all the difference in how you characterize the person. Someone who shouts or yells or calls out is a far different person than the one who squeaks, screeches, or pleads.

Be careful of the words you use to describe your hero or heroine and the reactions you give them. When new writers are trying to gain sympathy or show a character's suffering, they often include a lot of crying. Crying reduces the character's status in the eyes of the reader. Can you see Sarah Connor crying—or would she just jump in and take on the Terminator? Can you see Lady Mary showing weakness or wringing her hands? Never. If a dude dies in her bed at Downton Abbey, she just gets a maid to help drag him out.

Word choices are everything. Reactions characterize. Use them wisely.

EXERCISES

1. Play with subtext, and write a scene of dialogue in which the characters are implying something other than the words they are speaking.
2. Take notice of what you're revealing unintentionally in your work. Ask for opinions. Be sure you're not wearing out the reader or turning him away with subtext.

PART SIX
DRAWING EMOTIONS FROM CHARACTERS

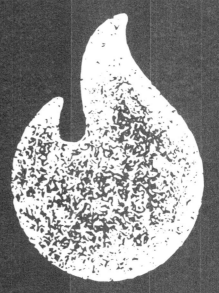

[24]
CHARACTER AS A COMPASS FOR EMOTIONS

Movies to watch: *While You Were Sleeping,*

Bridesmaids (R)

66 99

Story is honorable and trustworthy; plot is shifty, and best kept under house arrest. ... The best stories always end up being about the people rather than the event, which is to say character driven.

—STEPHEN KING, *ON WRITING: A MEMOIR OF THE CRAFT*

WHOSE STORY IS THIS?

Great characters remain with us long after the last page is turned. When you think back over your "keeper" books, it's the story people who stuck with you: Scarlet and Rhett in *Gone with the Wind*, Anne in *Anne of Greene Gables*, Christy and Fairlight Spencer in *Christy*, Jane Eyre and Edward Rochester in *Jane Eyre*, Atticus Finch in *To Kill a Mockingbird*, Clarice Starling and Hannibal Lecter in *The Si-*

lence of the Lambs. Those story people became so real to us that we remember them still.

The elements of story are so closely entwined that it's difficult to make a firm delineation where one aspect leaves off and another begins. Character and conflict are nothing without each other. Emotion and character go hand in hand. How a writer goes about developing characters is personal preference, and we need to use the methods that work for us. If you've studied something like The Hero's Journey (as identified by Joseph Campbell) and it's working for you, then by all means continue. If a character arc helps you flesh out story people, that's the method you should be incorporating.

Creating unforgettable characters is a technique that can be learned. The most believable characters are most often created by telling a story you're burning to tell. If it's a book *you'd* want to read, the characters who populate it are undoubtedly special.

A few things to remember:

- Characters are not real people. They need motivation to do what they do.
- Perfect characters are boring.
- By the end of the book, the character must have grown—also known by some as the character arc.
- Enrich each character with dialogue, individual to him or her.
- Be aware of your own strengths and weaknesses and make good use of them. If you write dynamite dialogue, use it to characterize. If revealing emotion is your forté, write scenes to enhance your character's feelings.
- How the character sees himself is as important as his worldview—maybe more.

How do you create a memorable character?

In *Bridesmaids*, Annie Walker has many flaws, but she's funny, sympathetic, and most of all lovable in her own quirky way. Her egotistical user boyfriend doesn't make her feel good about herself. She's broke; she has a failed business, two horrible roommates, and an old beater of a car; and she only has her sales job due to her mother's connections. Her life is already unraveling when her best friend Lillian gets engaged to a nice, successful man. Lillian's engagement leaves Annie feeling deserted, awkward, and lonelier than ever. She doesn't see herself as a desirable person or one worth spending time with or deserving of love. But she's proud and covers her pain with bravado.

Enter Helen, Lillian's boss's rich, pampered wife. Annie and Helen square off for Lillian's affections. Helen plans a fancy engagement party, and Annie plans the bridal-party luncheon and shopping—a disaster. Annie mocks Helen while driving home alone and is pulled over by Officer Rhodes. Rhodes is interested in Annie, but even after they get to know each other and spend a night together, Annie sabotages the relationship. She doesn't feel as though she deserves a good guy. Good things are out of her comfort zone; bad things are status quo. Annie has a lot of growing to do throughout this film. She and the odd collection of characters are memorable.

As writers we decide which traits to give our characters. We decide who these people are, and then we plan scenes and events that showcase those traits. Whether our characters are organized, controlling, quirky, or lonely, we must develop scenes to portray how we want the reader to perceive them. For example, simply saying that a character is sad and showing them crying is not enough to engage your reader's emotions. We need to experience the pain along with the character. First, we must understand the source of pain, see the character struggle with it, know the details, and watch how the character reacts.

Sacrifice is always endearing. How many heroes take a bullet for someone else? An anonymous gift or dismissal of a debt goes a long way. Forgiveness is seen as sacrifice, though it's beneficial to both persons.

Self-control is always a desirable quality. The character's action might be to turn the other cheek. He might have the physical strength and the motivation to rip the other guy apart, but backing away displays strength of character.

Have you ever noticed how the most compelling and creepiest villains take their time? They're not frantic and fumbling. Alan Rickman's calm, deadly politeness as Hans Gruber in *Die Hard* is the mark of the quintessential villain. To give someone more control and power, slow him down.

After seeing how many people listed *While You Were Sleeping* as one of their favorite Christmas movies—the movie has nearly a five-star average rating on Amazon—I gave it another watch to understand what causes viewers to connect with the film so strongly on an emotional level. It wasn't difficult to figure out why or to see how the writers made the connection.

Lucy Moderatz remembers being with her dad and the stories he told her about her mother. Lucy says, "She gave me the world," meaning an old globe she still treasures. Working at a tollbooth, Lucy sees Peter Callaghan every day and, without ever speaking to him, she falls in love with him. With no family, Lucy feels lonely and invisible, which is shown when she gives her landlord a Christmas gift and he doesn't reciprocate and when the hot-dog guy doesn't remember her "usual" but remembers her boss Jerry's "usual." Lucy is employee of the month during December because, with no family, she works holidays.

We are shown her life as usual: She selects a Christmas tree, which she decorates deliberately and precisely all alone, and goes to work, where she sees families taking trips. The setup is in place when Peter tells her "Merry Christmas." As she thinks to herself that she's going to marry that man, he is mugged and knocked off the platform. She rolls him to safety before a train hits him.

Once at the hospital, the rest is a comedy of mistaken identity. A nurse overhears Lucy mumble to herself, "I was going to marry him," so when the family shows up—an assorted cast of lovable nuts—the nurse tells them Lucy is Peter's fiancé. From there, the lie of omission snowballs until it's out of control. With Peter's family she's not invisible or alone. They welcome her to the family. She enjoys something she's never had, and nobody can blame her.

Watch this movie again, paying attention to details, character reactions, and emotional involvement.

The character is not you.

That statement might sound like a no-brainer, but I want you to think about it. Have you ever read multiple books by an author where the new protagonist in each seemed just like the one before? I've heard a lot of readers say, "I can't read Alice Author's books because she just changes the names and writes the same thing over and over again." Have you ever had a concern about making this mistake?

We do put a lot of ourselves into each and every book, and of course our stories pour from our individual wealth of knowledge and our worldviews. But our characters are not us and therefore cannot always think and act and react the way we do. We love it when we're watching a television show or a movie and the characters are behaving in completely unexpected and unfamiliar ways. Sometimes it's uncomfortable to watch. Sometimes we wish we could get into that character's head and fix their thinking.

But fix it to what? The way *we* think? The way *we* would behave and react? Why? Because it's more comfortable. Resist the urge to create characters with whom you are completely comfortable. You don't want to create cookie-cutter versions of yourself. Opposites attract, not only for couples, but for friendships, partnerships—and for the sake of interest. Think of it like this for a minute:

Remember in grade school when the captains were appointed during gym class and then picked teams? This selection process wasn't done randomly. The captain first selected the best person for the job. If it was softball, she picked the best batter, then the best catcher, and so on until only the nonathletes remained. Think of any group of people, and you will find that it is made up of an interesting mix of personality types, of people with diverse skills, beliefs, and habits.

Look at the Callaghan family in *While You Were Sleeping*, and see how endearing they are because of their quirky personalities and differences.

Let's take a look at the characters in *Friends*, one of the most popular sitcoms of all time, consistently ranked in the top ten primetime ratings.

* Rachel Green, fashion enthusiast, Monica Geller's best friend from childhood, waitress at a coffeehouse, later an assistant buyer at Bloomingdale's, later a buyer at Ralph Lauren
* Monica Geller, mother hen, chef, perfectionist, bossy, competitive, overweight as a child
* Phoebe Buffay, eccentric, a masseuse, self-taught musician, ditsy, street smart, writes and sings, has an evil twin
* Joey Tribbiani, struggling actor, food lover, simple minded, womanizer, innocent and caring, has good intentions
* Chandler Bing, statistical-analyst executive, later turned junior advertising copywriter, sarcastic sense of humor, bad luck in relationships
* Ross Geller, Monica's older brother, paleontologist, later a professor, sweet natured, good humored, clumsy, socially awkward, jealous and paranoid in relationships

The contrast in these characters' lives and personalities obviously kept things interesting for ten popular seasons.

The Big Bang Theory is another show that hosts a cast of diverse and interesting characters. While the men in this circle have much in common, they are made up of complex personalities. Their neighbor Penny is the complete opposite of them.

M*A*S*H was an entity unto itself in its day, with two leading protagonists supported by a large cast of diverse and entertaining personalities.

You will choose your main characters based on their ability to make the story conflict work to its fullest and then diversify characters as you bring in more.

Clip photos of men, women, and children from magazines and catalogs and store them in a file folder or binder. You might want to take it a step further and attach personality traits, education, and quirks to each photo until you have a cast of characters. Keep your collection handy to draw from when you need to develop a character or add a new person to your story.

Watch one of these movies:

- *While You Were Sleeping*
- *Bridesmaids*

Takes notes on how the main characters were brought onstage in character and the traits that were developed. Also take notes on the secondary characters and how they contrast with the main characters.

[25]
WHAT'S IN A NAME?

As writers we are in control of our story world and our characters. We are responsible for bringing characters to life as well as giving them believable names that will identify them and become a part of their overall makeup. A name *becomes* a character. You would be hard-pressed to find someone who doesn't have a visual image of Forrest Gump, Hannibal Lecter, or Mary Poppins. A name should reflect the personality of the character, sound natural, and also be memorable.

NAMING YOUR CHARACTERS

Choose a name worthy of this character, and make the character worthy of the name.

My stories don't begin to unfold until I've named my characters and named them correctly. How do I know if a name is "right"? I can't explain it. If their name is right, I can see the character. I can hear her talk. I can create scenes and situations for her. If a name is wrong, the character doesn't exist yet and I don't yet have a story. The character's name has to fit her so I can picture her.

I use a stack of books and my name binder to find character names. I keep lists of everything, so of course I have lists of names I want to use. Where do I get my lists of names? Obviously I'm an avid movie watcher, and I also check out new television shows. If I sit with a notebook and a pen, I can call it work. So I watch every line of the credits and write down names I like. It's research.

I save graduation programs, school band programs, and baby-name books. I've come home from many a burial service with names from gravestones written on the back of my memorial folder. If you browse your local Friends of the Library used-book sales, you can find vintage registers and books about county and state officers, townships, and so on filled with names. These books often include maps with street names and businesses.

I have over a dozen books of names, everything from baby names to character names with ethnic origins to names with their associated biblical meanings to pet names. The most popular names throughout history are listed at www.babycenter.com. You can also find popular names for any year after 1879 on the Social Security Administration website, www.ssa.gov. It's a pretty amazing feat of record keeping. For example, in 1888 the most popular baby names were John and Mary—a useful fact if you're writing a story set in that time period.

The Social Security site is invaluable for making sure your names are age appropriate for your characters. If you have a ninety-year-old woman in your story, you probably don't want to give her a name like Mackensie. Figure out her birth year and find an appropriate name.

I don't care for frivolous names or names that are difficult to pronounce. Even if I'm not reading aloud, I want to be able to know how to pronounce a name correctly. Fantasy and science fiction names are often exotic or unusual, but they still need to be easy to read and pronounce. Great examples include Bilbo Baggins, Aayla Secura, and Alpha Centauri. Some writers choose names by definition or meaning. Choosing a name symbolic of the character's role adds subtext.

Once I've chosen a character's name, the first name almost never changes; sometimes the last name will change as I introduce more people to the story. Naming secondary characters takes almost as much work. You shouldn't have two character names that sound alike, like Charlotte and Charlene or Monique and Monica or even David and Dennis, because it's confusing to the reader if two characters' names are similar or their names start with the same letter. We don't want our readers to rethink or have to go back and identify this person and be jerked out of the story.

Here's how I easily and simply prevent confusion with names: I keep a 5" × 7" index card with all the characters' names on it. At the bottom I write the alphabet. Every time I use a letter in a first or last name, I put a strike through a letter. Of course, as the story populates, I often use a letter two or three times, but some are for last names and others for secondary characters who won't be mixed up. Name endings must also differ. For example, you wouldn't want Whitley and Rigby and Riley appearing in the same scene—they all contain the "y" sound at the end.

If you prefer, you can create a file on your computer for this information. If you're writing a series, it's imperative to keep good track of names and include traits, a brief description, and even the page number in the manuscript where you described a particular character. This can be incorporated into your style sheet later.

Heritage, nationality, and connotation are as important as era. I would never name a high-powered female executive Trixie. I probably wouldn't name a nuclear physicist Tiffany. No offense to any nuclear physicists named Tiffany, but a scientist with this name would pull many readers out of the story. Tiffany is a teenager's best friend. On the other hand, you can go against stereotype by naming an enormous woman Daisy or a tiny dog Rambo. And keep in mind that many names automatically make you think of someone else: Rhianna, Orlando, Sly, Madonna, Britney, Cher, and Rizzo, to name a few.

Most important for me is that a character's name sounds like a real person's name, a real person I'd want to know. It must be a name that I won't mind typing hundreds of times.

I sometimes get stalled in the planning stages or first chapters of my story. In these cases, the story person's name is nagging at me because I was never quite sold on it. Once I rethink and change his name, the story moves on. I once revised a story proposal, removing the hero and replacing him with someone else. I was completely stumped for a name and couldn't develop the guy. I held a contest on my blog to name him. I knew the right name as soon as I saw it. With his name in place, the character sprang to life.

In my novella *Christmas in Red Willow* in the *Western Winter Wedding Bells* anthology, my heroine is Chloe Hanley. She's a determined and pretty young thing. Her only family was her grandfather before he died. She has a boarder, Miss Sarah Wisdom, who plays the piano every evening and is persnickety in all her ways. Owen Reardon is a carpenter, a second son with a big, loud family, who is slow to speak and likes to keep to himself. His bossy, know-it-all brother is Richard, and his down-to-earth, matchmaking mother is Lillith.

In *Song of Home,* my heroine Ruby Dearing left home at sixteen to have an adventure. Her sister Pearl stayed home and took care of their ailing mother. The hero is Nash Sommerton, and he's also … her dead sister's widower. He has turned the Dearing farm into a ranch and now has no intention of turning it over to anyone as irresponsible as Ruby. When I first started working on the story, I had named the hero Finn. Nothing would come together, and I was thoroughly frustrated. I just didn't have a handle on him. But after changing his name—twice—the plot fell into place.

A lot of writers select names by their meanings or derivations. Most baby-name books are accompanied by their respective meanings. *The Writer's Digest Character Naming Sourcebook* is one resource I like because it divides characters by nationality. If you want a book chock-full of lists of everything from eye shape to body language, check out Mac McCutcheon's *The Writer's Digest Sourcebook for Building Believable Characters.*

I create a style sheet for each book, which is a page or two that I turn in with the manuscript. The style sheet contains a list of all the character names and all the places, streets, businesses, and proper nouns in the story. This reference helps me create the story and also helps the copyeditor. And it sure comes in handy when I do a sequel.

EXERCISES

1. If you haven't already, start your own list, book, or binder of names. If you're opposed to paper, create files on your computer or use PBworks online.

2. If you need prompts to come up with character traits, do a Google search for positive and negative character traits or enneagram (see chapter 27) personalities and fatal flaws.

3. Try this exercise for right-brain creativity: Tear out a photo of a person from a magazine. Tear out another photo that represents this person's home.

   Answer these questions about the person:
   • What one thing motivates him?
   • What is his one happiest memory?
   • What is his one worst nightmare?

   Now name him.

[26]
WHERE DO GREAT CHARACTERS COME FROM?

Movie to watch: *Die Hard*

Great characters are born from the minds and hearts of great writers. Our most important job is to wrest feelings from the reader. Strong emotions can be created by those "givens" I referred to previously. Examples of favorable givens can be children, animals, parent-child love, sibling loyalty, grandparents, orphans, and underdogs. Any of these factors come with built-in preconceived beliefs—and therefore feelings.

Underdog or fish-out-of-water characters are one of my favorite character types and can be developed in limitless ways. Here's a guy you might not think of as an underdog until you look more closely: John McClane in *Die Hard*. From the beginning we see his fear of flying, which is a small flaw. He's anxious about spending Christmas with his wife, Holly, from whom he's estranged. He loves her and wants to get back together with her. He's a fish out of water at the Nakatomi office party. We already sympathize with him, more so than if he'd been a confident, suave fellow. He's endearing, even though he's a rule breaker with a resentful attitude. The rest of the movie is about John saving Holly, even if he has to walk on broken glass with bare feet. He's a flawed hero, and we root for him the entire way.

Unfavorable givens are bullies, infidelity, physical and mental abuse, oppression, death, and unfairness. Think about villains you dislike the most and situations that make you the most uncomfortable. Which characters have you felt sorry for? Back in the day I read Janelle Taylor's Ecstasy series with tears running down my cheeks because she evoked strong emotion with vivid writing and endearing characters.

If you're serious about learning to use emotion, first learn about yourself and the things that affect you deeply. Make a list of the books and movies that made you laugh or cry and left a lasting impression. List the reasons why.

Look inside yourself for the situations and qualities that move you, and create new ones. How many of the things that evoke emotion in you are givens? How many were created? A good many people get teary at Hallmark commercials. They may be sixty seconds worth of manipulation, but the creators pull out all the stops to make us feel emotional over the sentiment of giving and receiving a greeting card.

Invented or created emotions come from carefully structured motivation. We manipulate the readers' feelings with characters and incidents about which they can feel strongly and circumstances with which they can identify.

LEAVE A LASTING IMPRESSION ON THE READER

A story without strong emotion is not a story brought to life. Editors are looking for depth, color, and fire. They're seeking emotional connections that make the book memorable.

In the Harlequin "So You Think You Can Write" forum, editor Leslie Wainger said:

> Before a reader can be engaged by your story, you
> have to be engaged by it, and the best books are those

that won't leave you alone before they ever get the chance to haunt a reader (or your editor). But the next step—the step that so often separates the pros from the hopefuls—comes with your ability to think about why a particular idea fascinates you and how you can make it equally fascinating to the reader.

When we look back at the books we've loved the most, it's the characters we recall most vividly. We can picture them and hear them speaking. Close your eyes for a few minutes, and think of those stories that captured your heart forever. Who populated the pages? Jo March from *Little Women*, Colonel Christopher Brandon in *Sense and Sensibility*, Augustus McCrae in my personal favorite, *Lonesome Dove*? You remember these characters from the way they made you feel.

A long time ago, I heard this quote from Maya Angelou, and I never forgot it. In fact I've lived by the words: "At the end of the day, people won't remember what you said or did; they will remember how you made them feel."

It's true. I don't recall conversations word for word. I remember the gist of what the person told me and how it made me feel. Think back over your life and the things that shaped you. How did gym class make you feel? What about your sixth-grade math teacher? How did your grandmother or grandfather make you feel? Where were you when your candidate was elected, when your first child was born, or when the Twin Towers fell? You remember exactly because of how people and events make you feel. Similarly we want to leave strong impressions with our readers.

Leslie Wainger went on to say, "And as an editor, I'm looking for the best books. I'm not saying that you should avoid popular hooks or unpredictable twists. What I'm saying is that inherent in your idea should be characters who can believably and compellingly take you in [any] direction because it's characters who keep a reader invested."

So often when we see how-to instructions on creating characters, we're given character tag suggestions and empty lines for physical description. "Her long hair in a copper braid" and "his wide-legged stance" give us visual images, which are necessary and important. Descriptions carry texture and add concrete images, but alone they create story people we can see but with whom we can't identify because we don't know what makes them tick or why we should identify with them.

Many times beginning writers think that giving a character a quirk or a mannerism is characterization. It's not. Yes, small things like phrases or body language individualize a person, but they aren't the compelling factors needed to wholeheartedly help us engage. *The Closer* was a popular television show that won many awards in its seven-year run, but I never believed Deputy Chief Brenda Leigh Johnson's character because she was over-the-top quirky. Besides an accent and an attitude, she was a terrible driver and apparently had a chocolate-eating disorder. All those tags made her too comical for me to buy into her as a woman to be taken seriously.

Believable, memorable characters are complicated combinations of pride and vulnerabilities, appealing mixes of dashing and determined exteriors with hurts, hopes, and dreams—like yours.

Bring the character on "in character."

When I introduce a character, I first choose his most important trait. He will have many to round him out, but this is the trait I want the reader to see first—the impression I want this character to make.

In the *Writer's Digest* article "Allow Me to Introduce ..." Kevin J. Anderson wrote, "If you can't decide which technique would best introduce each character, imagine how you'd present that character's real-life equivalent to a roomful of people. You might say, 'This is the aunt who taught me everything I know about raising children,' or pat your brother on the back while speaking in a watch-out-for-him tone or present a nodding acquaintance with a quick, 'This is Mr. So-and-So.'"

In my novel *Saint or Sinner*, my heroine Addie has a secret that shaped her into who she is today. We don't learn her secret until chapter 4, but meanwhile, we learn the things she holds dear and speculate about what made her this way.

Adelaide Stapleton snapped a heavy, wet sheet and pinned it to the clothesline with faultless precision. Comfortable with the routine, she inspected the sheet's pristine whiteness with a critical eye and glanced across the sloping expanse of side yards, assuring herself her laundry was, as usual, the first out this sunny Monday morning in mid-April.

She ignored the fact that the other women of Van Caster, Indiana, had families to feed and babies to dress before they began their chores, and simply derived satisfaction from setting a good example. Addie clipped a pair of violet-embroidered pillow slips beside her sheets. Tomorrow she would iron them.

Wednesdays she did the mending she took in. Her income from that, as well as a moderate amount of dressmaking and selling her jams and jellies, earned enough to keep her small home running comfortably. There was never enough for extras, but Addie didn't need extras. Her little house and garden, and her friends in town, were all she needed.

On Thursdays she led the ladies mission society, the Dorcas Society, in Bible study, prayer and quilt-making. Fridays she tied a scarf over her thick gold hair, hung her rugs on the clothesline and beat them with a wire rug beater. She performed the chore with such enthusiasm and regularity that dust never dared settle in the oval rows of braided fabric. While the rugs aired, Addie scrubbed and polished her square-roomed little house until it fairly sparkled.

Saturday's routine called for baking and putting up her preserves. And on Sunday, of course, Adelaide Stapleton arrived at the schoolhouse early, arranged the benches and the hymnals, and welcomed the circuit preacher, should Van Caster be so fortunate as to have Reverend Moorehead visit that month. And if not, like yesterday, she and the townspeople sang a few songs and read from their Bibles.

The families would disperse afterward, going home for Sunday dinner and their highly overrated relaxation. On Sunday afternoons in winter, Addie sewed baby clothing and crocheted hats, sweaters and booties to sell to Demetris Bentley at the mercantile. Spring's arrival warmed her heart, for in fair weather she spent Sunday afternoons gardening.

Being an important part of this little town gave her the stability she craved. Nobody remembered that Addie hadn't always been part of the community, and that suited her fine. If she'd had her way, she would have been born and raised among these people and their modest homes and businesses. Too bad the good Lord didn't give a body the choice of where to come into the world. Roots were important to Addie, and she had sunk hers deep here in Van Caster.

Addie sandwiched her undergarments between two lines of sheets and towels. Not that anyone had ever come by on Monday, but a lady must observe the proprieties at all times. The sound of a wagon arrested her attention, and she turned, lifting a hand over her brow against the morning sun.

A dog barked. Addie spotted the enormous animal bounding along the muddy road ahead of a wagon: the dog was a dirty yellow color with shaggy hair and mud caked up all four legs. The canine caught sight of her and, tail wagging and ears flopping, cleared her forsythia bushes in an eager leap. Addie realized the dog's destination at the same time the man driving the wagon hollered.

"Cully!"

Tongue lolling out the side of its mouth, the dog bore down on her.

"Cully, stop!" Losing his hat, the man jumped from the wagon seat and loped after the approaching dog.

Ignoring him, the bad-mannered Cully closed the distance, gave a joyous yelp and jumped up at Addie. "No! Down!" she cried.

Enormous paws struck her chest, and she turned on her way down in an attempt to deflect the slobbering attack. She only rerouted the muddy paws from the front of her dress to the nearest white sheet.

"Oh!" Addie plopped into her wicker basket, scattering her remaining underclothes. The sheet pulled loose from the line with the animal's considerable weight and, running from the man, Cully dragged the wet linen across the yard on his back.

Addie managed to extricate herself from the basket and sit up, hurriedly pulling her skirts down over her stockinged legs. The tall, dark-haired man chased the dog until he caught up with her sheet and carried it back to her with an irritating lack of repentance gracing his disturbingly handsome face.

"Ma'am." He shifted the sheet beneath one arm and reached his other hand down to her. "Let me help you up."

"I can do it." Addie scrambled to her feet and reached for her intimate laundry.

The impression I wanted to give the reader was of Addie's perfectionism and the extreme importance of her stable, routine life. Hell-raiser Joshua McBride's arrival in town knocks her off kilter, and after we learn her secret, we know why she fights him tooth and nail and why it's so important for her to be seen as a pillar in the community.

Addie is determined and stubborn yet incredibly vulnerable. She spends every waking moment working on her poor self-image and falling short of who she wants to be. She tells herself she's strong and capable—and she is—but she is also fragile.

Addie knows what she wants, and those desires are very clear in the introductory paragraphs. She needs to keep her life on an even keel. She needs to feel that life is safe and orderly. She needs to be respected. Over our lifetimes we unconsciously develop coping mechanisms to help us avoid pain or deny unpleasantness. These coping mechanisms can improve or distort our self-image, and Addie shares our common need to feel better about ourselves.

I went to Amazon to find a reader comment about the book. Here's what I found:

> This was the first book of Cheryl's that I read ... that was all it took. Now I am hooked. It was a story like no other I had read. It was a story filled with love, danger, and intrigue ... it just touches the heart and sets fire to the soul. Cheryl is a talented lady, and it was this book, which I read when I was fifteen, that inspired me to write my own novel. She has a talent that is not always found in most novels ... a talent that keeps me hooked from page one. I cannot for anything—even to eat—put down one of her books before I have read it completely. This is her best work. The characters Joshua and Adelaide are done to perfection. They come to life through her carefully chosen words. The characters and their story remain in your mind and in your heart long after you have finished the book.

Presenting characters in a way that makes the reader connect should be our goal for each and every book we set out to write. I believe it's the characters that make readers fall in love with Addie's story. It's the way this book makes them feel.

To know that something I wrote inspired a young person to write brings me indescribable joy. I'm both honored and humbled, and I'm convinced we can use proven techniques to make readers love our characters. It's not easy—nothing about writing is easy. There are no shortcuts to this sometimes tedious or frustrating process, but with determination and the right tools, we can create memorable characters and take pride in a job well done.

It's what's inside that counts.

Introduce an emotional flaw within the first few chapters, and do it delicately. Don't dump the character backstory on the reader because the reader isn't invested yet. Rather, show the character in an interesting way, and show his emotional flaw. In the excerpt from *Saint or Sinner*, you saw that Addie needed to control her life, have a solid, unbendable schedule, and have others look up to her as upstanding and virtuous. The reader doesn't learn the full impact of her backstory until a few chapters later, and then her behavior becomes completely justified and believable. In chapter 22 I explained how the creators of *Longmire* showed Walt's character flaws with subtlety while at the same time making us care. Much of storytelling is finessing how much to tell, what to hold back, and how to show something without hitting the reader over the head with it.

Readers want to become emotionally involved with your story—that's why they paid for your book. They must feel the story in order to buy into the premise and turn the pages, and they must have a good experience in order to buy your next book.

EXERCISE

Search online for a list of character flaws, and pick one for your character. Make a list of ways you will show this flaw, and plan how your character will grow.

If you have a villain, how can the villain use this flaw against your character?

[27]
THE READER MUST CARE

Movie to watch: *Rain Man*

MAKE THE READER CARE

The characters make or break the book, and the strength of a character can be everything. You can have the cleverest plot ever and use perfect grammar, but if you don't create people your audience will identify with and root for—or hate, as the case may be—you don't have a book worthy of publication.

How do you make the reader care? Give your character believable traits and flaws. Imperfections and weaknesses make a character more realistic and appealing to us, like John McClane in *Die Hard*. Flaws make a person human because we all have flaws. Another flawed character we root for is Charlie Babbitt in *Rain Man*. In this film we start out thinking the character is a real jerk because of his selfish qualities, but as the story progresses and we see his interaction with people—people he loves—a whole person emerges and we are hooked in for the story and resolution.

Bottom line: We care what happens.

In *Rain Man*, Charlie is a self-involved, materialistic hustler with rigid emotional defenses. He remembers an imaginary playmate who turns out to be his autistic savant brother, Raymond. His one happy childhood memory is of the Rain Man who sang to him when he was frightened. After the death of their mother, Raymond was placed in a home, and their father pretended Raymond didn't exist. Charlie has been wounded by a father who couldn't show love. His vulnerability is well hidden, yet we find him sympathetic. When he was sixteen, he and his father had a falling out over a vintage Buick and Charlie left home. He avoids emotional involvement.

His goal is to sell his cars, get his inheritance, and save his business. Charlie thinks getting his 1.5 million dollar inheritance will solve his problems and make him happy. He will do everything in his power to get Raymond to Los Angeles and establish guardianship. He's quick-witted and charming in getting exactly what he needs to accomplish his goal. He's a survivor, but he can't manipulate Raymond like he does everyone else. Everything that follows is an obstacle: Raymond, Susanna, Dr. Bruner, and the unsympathetic bankers.

You must lay out a natural, believable development in even increments to show why your character is compelled to change—and that he's capable of change. Stimuli for growth come both from the outside and the inside. Charlie's external conflict mirrors his internal conflict.

Raymond's idiosyncrasies create problems for Charlie. His refusal to get on the plane, his insistence on eating certain foods on certain days, and his avoidance of touch all hinder the journey, but through the series of events, Charlie gains an understanding of his brother. Raymond sings "I Saw Her Standing There," and Charlie joins him. Charlie learns Raymond was the one who comforted him as a child. He discovers that his father's fear that Raymond would hurt Charlie caused Raymond to be institutionalized for twenty years. Because of these things, Charlie's bitterness fades and his attitude toward Raymond changes.

The brothers pretend to be high rollers in Vegas. Raymond learns to dance. These are increments in Charlie's growth and change. Getting to know Raymond teaches Charlie selflessness and generosity. Charlie says, "I had a father I hardly knew, a mother I didn't know at all. I found out a few days ago that I have a brother, and I want to be with him." We see Charlie learn forgiveness and compassion. Eventually he gives up his fight for the inheritance. He admits Walbrook is the best place for Raymond and abandons his custody battle. Through the journey he also realizes he needs Susanna. Tough guy Charlie recognizes his need for family.

Selfishness and greed don't have to be reserved for villains only, but use them with care and planning. Show how your character came to this place and how he feels. Charlie had plenty of motivation for callousness, bitterness, and a need to control. His self-serving attitude is the result of survival instincts, but Charlie redeems himself as he develops understanding and love for his brother. A character who learns nothing and never grows throughout the story process is hopelessly flawed and fodder for villain material.

The movie *Rain Man* won us over with characterization. Character development only works if the characters overcome or win in the story journey.

MAKE THE READER BELIEVE

When I read a book, I must be convinced that the character is the sort of person who would be doing what he is doing. We would never have thought Indiana Jones was believable if he had unhesitatingly jumped into that pit of snakes to rescue the girl.

Give your characters believable motivations. Show enough of your character's background and the forces that shaped her so that the reader can accept her actions, fears, and goals. This means extensive, consistent documentation of the kind of person she is. A heroine who watched her parents die in a blaze will not readily run into a burning building, but she will overreact when the hem of her skirt catches fire.

Know every internal need and emotion. Don't be so busy making character charts on favorite colors and foods that you don't know each and every nuance of what makes up your character's emotions and inner struggles.

In these paragraphs, Sherri Shackelford, author of *The Marshal's Ready-Made Family*, gives us a peek at the character's low opinion of herself through dialogue:

"Would you mind very much if I had a scar?" JoBeth chuckled, attempting to lighten the somber mood. "Would you be upset if I was ugly?"

Garrett jolted upright. "You could never be ugly."

"I could never be pretty."

"That's because pretty is for debutantes and silly girls. You're beautiful."

Resentment welled in her chest. "I'm not. And I'll sock you for teasing me."

"Don't you call me a liar, Miss JoBeth McCoy." Garrett cupped the side of her face with his warm hand and studied her bandaged cheek. "Do you know why Tom is so mean to you?"

"Because I made him look like a fool in front of his friends."

"Nope." Garrett removed the warmth of his hand. "Because you broke his heart."

"I think you musta hit your head last night."

"Don't forget, I was a young man once too. I know the signs."

"I sure wasn't Tom's first anything."

"Did he ever try and kiss you?" Garrett asked with a knowing grin.

"Once. I stomped on his toe."

"That's your proof. A man will forgive being made a fool of, but he never forgets his first love."

Jo scoffed. "If he had a crush on me, wouldn't he be nice?"

"Boys aren't always good at knowing what to do with their feelings."

Her head spun with his words and she latched onto his earlier comment. "Who was your first love?"

"I never had one."

"Then you don't really know for certain. And you're wrong about Tom. He's told me I'm ugly a thousand times."

"I'm right." Garrett declared. "And someday I'll prove it to you. Just like I'll finally make you realize how beautiful you are."

"Quit foolin' with me."

"For a smart woman, you're awfully dumb about some things."

Compare and contrast.

Everything needs something by which to measure it in order to know how important it is.

Make the reader believe by utilizing your character's self-image. Who does your character compare himself to? Whose yardstick does he use to measure himself? How does he compensate for feelings of inadequacy or past mistakes?

In a classic favorite of mine, Laura Kinsale's *The Shadow and the Star*, Leda measures herself with the South Street Ladies yardstick. Raised in a circle of fading widows and well-bred spinsters, surrounded by their demure, principled little society, she grew to womanhood seeing herself as the not-quite-respectable daughter of a Frenchwoman. Viewing herself as half French justifies a score of emotions and actions: drinking wine, succumbing to her attraction for Samuel, enjoying his kisses and touches. That she is half French matters to no one but her.

Samuel, who believes he doesn't deserve her respect because of his own self-image, asks if she respects him even after he kisses her crudely. She replies, "Yes. Even that, because—I am half French, you see." The reader must laugh. And Samuel? "…What being half French had to do with it he didn't hope to understand. It was just Leda, she would say such things, nonsense and innocence—stubborn, gentle, resolute, oblivious innocence…."

But the reader understands and loves Leda because we know her self-image.

GOING FOR THE HEART OR THE JUGULAR

In *Her Colorado Man*, Wes has come to Colorado, pretending and wanting to be John James's father. This is a scene of reflection in which Wes compares his own childhood to the lives of the children in the Spangler's home.

Both of the boys' beds were draped with down coverlets. Thick woven rugs covered the floor. Low shelves under the window held an assortment of toys.

In the darkness, Wes's gaze touched on each of their slight forms. His thoughts traveled back over twenty some years to his childhood. To the long stark room where he'd slept at the foundling home.

Bedtime had been a dismal affair, especially in winter when the children bundled in their threadbare stockings and union suits and still weren't warm. A shrilling bell had clanged in the hallway, notifying them when it was time to undress and get into bed. It had rung again, the signal that they'd best be lying down.

The principal showed up then, a tall wiry man who always wore a black suit. He admonished them to go directly to sleep and straightaway he turned off the gas lamp on the wall, plunging the cold room into darkness.

Oftentimes the younger boys or the newly arrived cried themselves to sleep. Sometimes one of them said a quiet prayer, pleading with God for safety or clothing or...family.

Wes let his gaze touch each boy in this cozy warm room. Knowing these children would never experience hunger or loneliness or unworthiness gave him deep satisfaction. Their huge enveloping family would always see to it that they were loved and provided for. The fact that they didn't even recognize it—that they took this security for granted as the only manner life they knew—made the knowledge all the sweeter.

The only thing missing in John James's life had been a father. Wes didn't regret his decision to be that person for him.

But he wondered what that kind of security and love—what being wanted—felt like. John James was the only person who'd ever cared whether or not Wes stayed, the only one who'd looked at him as though he was someone important. Someone loved.

And for the first time Wes recognized the responsibility of having someone who cared for him. Accountability like this was foreign, but he liked it. He had more value in his own eyes because of this boy. He would never let him down.

Wes's backstory came into play by comparing and contrasting, and he's not only justifying what he's done but working around guilt.

YOUR CHARACTER MUST GROW

This is a fiction basic. In author speak this is known as the "come to realize" or the "CTR." The skilled writer provides the character enough adequate and convincing experiences throughout the story to give her a believable change of heart, but care must be taken. This eventual realization, or "come-to-realize" moment will seem contrived if she doesn't have the potential to change from the beginning and her motivation hasn't changed with the story events.

Knowing your character is a process. Any developing relationship takes time, and you must put effort into becoming intimate with this person. Once you've prepared the foundation, you must trust yourself to start the story, even if you aren't fully convinced you know this person well enough. Start anyway, understanding that you'll go back to those first pages and chapters again and again before the story is finished. Sometimes it takes three or more chapters before we are comfortable with a character. And sometimes you will get to the middle and realize a particular character said or did something at the beginning that he would never have done.

The character development process happens over the course of the story, not overnight. As you show your character reacting and making decisions, the whole person emerges. Your character's past, opinions, and beliefs are his core values and his worldview. They make him unique and believable, like Charlie Babbitt. The reader wants to believe.

BIRTH ORDER

Your character's birth order can play a big part in knowing who she is. The character traits for firstborns, youngest, middle children, and only children are different, and study in this area is often beneficial. There are good books out there, and I especially like Dr. Kevin Leman's *The Birth Order Book: Why You Are the Way You Are.*

ENNEAGRAMS

An enneagram is a diagram or an unbiased study of personality types implying attitudes and behaviors, capacities, and limitations influenced by childhood development. Enneagrams are an interesting study that can help you understand and develop characters.

- The Reformer is idealistic, principled, purposeful, self-controlled, and a perfectionist. He does everything the right way.
- The Helper is caring, interpersonal, demonstrative, generous, people-pleasing, and possessive. She must help others.
- The Achiever/Motivator is success oriented, pragmatic, adaptive, driven, image conscious. He must succeed.
- The Individualist/Romantic is sensitive, withdrawn, expressive, dramatic, self-absorbed, and temperamental. She is unique.
- The Investigator/Thinker is intense, cerebral, perceptive, innovative, secretive, and isolated. He must understand the world.
- The Loyalist/Skeptic is committed, security oriented, engaging, responsible, anxious, and suspicious. She is affectionate.
- The Enthusiast is busy, fun loving, spontaneous, versatile, distractible, and scattered. He is happy and open to new things.
- The Challenger/Leader is powerful, dominating, self-confident, decisive, willful, and confrontational. She must be strong.
- The Peacemaker is easygoing, self-effacing, receptive, reassuring, agreeable, and complacent. He is at peace.

How these personality types interact and work in relationships is an interesting study and well worth investigating.

Give your character a skill, and then use it. Let it come in handy. In *The Hunger Games*, Katniss possessed skill in bow hunting and it came in handy when she fought for her life. Han and Luke were great pilots, a handy skill when fighting off the Empire's bad guys and destroying the Death Star in *Star Wars*.

ORIGINALITY

Unless you can tweak and improve on one, avoid clichés. Details that are tired and overdone bore your reader and don't make for fascinating characters. We can spot the strong, silent type a mile away. He has a craggy face and a hard, chiseled jaw. If this is your guy, put a twist on him that nobody will see coming. Maybe he has a soft spot for animals or he collects miniature trains.

Most of us have met the preacher who is mad at God after a trauma. His wife was killed, and he's still blaming God years later. Struggling writers have been done to death. Richard Castle from the popular television show *Castle* is fun because he's successful at writing, and while he looks like a man, he acts more like a little boy most of the time. His daughter is the adult in their relationship. If you have never watched it, give yourself a treat to see how the writers made the character fresh.

The awkward kid who gets bullied is a standard. The exhausted med student has been around forever. The cynical cop is a norm—and John McClane might have been one if the writer hadn't changed him up and given him foibles and a love story.

As Solomon said, there is nothing new under the sun. It's all been done before. We've probably all heard that there are only seven basic plot archetypes, and every story we read and every movie is a derivation of one of these. This is basically true. What makes a story unique is the twist the writer gives the tale and the well-developed, interesting, and sympathetic characters within it.

We want our story people to be three-dimensional and act independently. They are not compilations of character traits we can move around in the story like paper dolls. They are *people* who are *experi-*

encing the story as we unfold it. The more we know about them, the more we develop them and give them their own story, the more they come to life. If we don't care about these people, then readers won't care about the story. It all comes back to Rule One: *A story is feelings.* Make the reader care.

EXERCISES

1. Recognize: Are you a plot-driven or character-driven writer and reader? Embrace your methods. Considering your personal style, direct the suggestions I've given you to make the reader care about your characters.

   - What does your character want on an emotional level?
   - How will he feel when he meets resistance?
   - Show this character suffering without oppressive word choices.
   - Show what happened in the character's past.
   - Write a scene about your character's internal dilemma.
   - Use deep point of view during a conversation.
   - Show how a character is misunderstood by someone.
   - Show your character's frustration.

2. Your character must leave quickly. In five minutes, he packs everything that's important into one small bag. Describe each item that goes into the bag, and tell why it's important. Have the character say something about one or two items.

[28]
TECHNIQUES TO MAKE THE READER CARE

GETTING DOWN TO BUSINESS

Every writer must find the method of character creation that works for her. Maybe those charts of eye colors, favorite foods, and songs are helpful to you; a lot of writers use them. A list of questions for each character can also be helpful.

- What does he want?
- What price will he pay?
- Why can't he have it?
- What is at stake?
- How does he feel about himself?
- What is his secret?
- What is his biggest regret?

You can even go into physical details, though they are not as important as emotional details or story conflict. Dig deeper into character and be consistent with this person's development.

As soon as I have an idea for a story, I sit down with a pen and spiral notebook and write down everything I know about the story and the people who will populate the pages. Sometimes my notes are several pages long. Other times I only have a few paragraphs. These are the first rough pages that go into my binder. Next comes brainstorming. I shake this idea upside down and sideways to see what falls out. I take the idea to my critique group, bounce it off their brains, and add more notes. My objective at this point is to make sure I have enough conflict to sustain these characters' story.

I officially start every book with the development of the characters, and I do so with forms I've created for this purpose. Because I plan goal, motivation, and conflict first, I create a GMC character sheet. Your characters are nothing without something to motivate them, a goal or two, and opposition.

GMC CHARACTER SHEET

For each main character, I write down:
- How the story will start and the moment of change
- Motivation: factors and incidents in backstory and the reasoning behind believable actions
- Long-term goal: springs from backstory and emotional needs
- Short-term goal: steps character will take to reach long-term goal
- Character flaw and a plan for how to use it against them
- Internal conflict: what drives them emotionally (For romance, I answer: "I can't love him because _____.")
- External conflict: the physical opposition
- Black moment: when the worst happens
- "Come to realize"/realization: Deliver on the promise in chapter 1; characters realize their flaws, and I've shown how they've grown.
- Theme: Ideally all characters are connected by the theme

Next comes my Character Prep Sheet. These are the stats I fill in for each character:

CHARACTER PREP SHEET

NAME:

AGE:

JOB OR POSITION

FAMILY

PERSONALITY

TEN DESCRIPTORS (ADJECTIVES)

1	6
2	7
3	8
4	9
5	10

HIS/HER STRONGEST TRAIT

HIS/HER WEAKEST TRAIT

HIS/HER GREATEST FEAR

INTERNAL MOTIVATION AND CONFLICT

Here are two examples from *The Preacher's Daughter*:

NAME: Lorabeth Holdridge

AGE: 20

JOB OR POSITION
Preacher's daughter; Caleb hired her two years ago; "social worker" personality

FAMILY
Preacher's daughter; grew up in a safe, strict, learning environment, watching for an opportunity to spread her wings

PERSONALITY
Hungry for love and affection; needs to feel special and be understood
Love and beauty interest her

TEN DESCRIPTORS (ADJECTIVES)

1. frustrated

2. idealistic, sensitive

3. passionate but restrained

4. stifled, eager for love and affection

5. imperfect

6. spontaneous

7. impulsive but holds it back

8. affectionate

9. curious

10. wholeheartedly sympathetic

Emotionally intense, helper, thirsty for *life*

HER STRONGEST TRAIT
Equanimity, peacemaker

HER WEAKEST TRAIT
Envy

HER GREATEST FEAR
She's only loved because she is perfect: "works"
Being misunderstood, being defective

INTERNAL MOTIVATION AND CONFLICT
Weary of striving for perfection
High expectations and visibility require much restraint
She had a perfect mother, but that didn't mean she felt loved
Feels she has more potential
Unrealized, understated, unappreciated potential

NAME: Benjamin Chaney

AGE: 24

JOB OR POSITION
Veterinarian

FAMILY
Ellie's brother, son of town prostitute
Dirt poor, abusive childhood, illegitimate child, doesn't know
who his father is

PERSONALITY
Old beyond his years, jaded
Kindhearted, abhors weakness, loves animals
Has very high standards for himself in the world

TEN DESCRIPTORS (ADJECTIVES)

1. kind-hearted	**6.** frustrated
2. self-improved, skilled, competent	**7.** tainted
3. ashamed	**8.** perfectionist, improver
4. educated at university	**9.** respectful
5. jaded	**10.** Stubborn— won't sell the house

HIS STRONGEST TRAIT

Self-control; it's all about control

HIS WEAKEST TRAIT

Unworthiness, anger—it's all inside

HIS GREATEST FEAR

Hurting or tainting a woman, losing control, being like the men he saw as a boy

INTERNAL MOTIVATION AND CONFLICT

Sees passion and desire as a weakness; puts a lot of energy into producing perfection

Single-handedly protecting women

I use my Goal, Motivation, Conflict sheet and Character Prep Sheets to write my synopsis every time, without fail. A synopsis must focus on why the character is doing what he's doing, and from my GMC and list of character traits, the story is already in place. Everything I need to build the bones of the story is right here.

If I need to tweak conflict or add more believable motivation, I spot it at this stage.

You might also want to add plot points, which are used in scriptwriting. Plot points are the high points in the drama. A plot point is often new information: A new person shows up who changes everything … the person we thought dead is alive … a letter arrives and changes the character's journey and goal. Plot points can appear in every third or fourth of the book. Mine are usually at each third. I look at how many pages or total words my story will be when completed, and I plan for a plot point one-third of the way through. At two-thirds through, another plot point appears that is more dramatic than the last. In a romance this can be a love scene—emotional or physical involvement changes everything. In a mystery, a body can show up or the sleuth can be kidnapped. The point is to escalate the events and keep the tension high and the outcome in question.

Once you design the elements that pull together your story most effectively, you will be able to develop characters thoroughly enough to devise a plot and write a synopsis before you start the story—or at least before you've gone further than three chapters. Writing a synopsis before the book would be a good goal to work toward if you don't already do this.

AS YOU'RE WRITING

Keep these prep sheets in your binder so you can refer back and stay focused. Add sheets for physical descriptions and names and photos to help you bring your story people to life.

Get inspired to know these characters and write this story. Find triggers to jumpstart you each time you sit down to work. Pick a theme song for your story.

Soundtracks work great if you can write with music. I usually need quiet to work, but sometimes I'm more inspired if I have music. I listen to a lot of movie soundtracks, instrumentals, Native American flute music, and piano pieces. Even forest sounds or water running can create a relaxing atmosphere. It can often help to select one particular soundtrack for a book and put it on each time you're ready to write. Celtic, Irish, Native

American, big band—whatever inspires you. You can download a Pandora app on your Kindle, phone, or computer and find channels that appeal to your creative side.

Hang up pictures that help you visualize your characters, and look at them often. Collect pictures of the cars they drive—or buggies, as the case may be—clothing, pets, rooms, their family and friends, and anything that puts you in the scene.

I love to collage. Some writers, like Jenny Crusie, go all out. Search online for her name and the word *collage,* and have a look at the amazing collections she puts together for each book. She creates three-dimensional masterpieces that she plans out and for which she purchases items at craft stores. Mine are simple clipped pictures, words, and photos glued on posterboard, but they fulfill the same purpose—fleshing out the story and giving me a visual jumpstart.

EXERCISE

Once you believe you've done the best job you can on the first three to five chapters of your manuscript, ask someone who has never seen it before to read it. Ask this person to take notes and let you know what she learned about the characters in each chapter, what emotions she felt, and at what points in the story she felt them. Ask for a list of questions and thoughts on the story. Consider all the remarks and questions, and place yourself in your reader's shoes. Analyze every scene with her questions and comments in mind.

WRAPPING IT UP

Years ago I read this quote, and it stayed with me: "You're only as good as your next book." That philosophy was eye opening and motivating. Years of publishing genre series fiction proved it. We promote, and we move on to the next project that inspires us. The growth of digital publishing has changed the longevity of a book because e-books have limitless shelf lives. Granted, a few authors live well off their laurels and the royalties of a blockbuster or a trilogy—especially if there are movie rights—but most of us are in it to build heavy backlists and produce new material.

I won't promise you that writing skills get easier the longer you've been at it. Yes, many of the techniques become second nature, but no two books are the same, and sometimes a method that worked for you in the past doesn't work for a new project. The more you write, however, the more you become aware of your own deficiencies, which helps you work toward a higher standard. Dwight V. Swain said in *Techniques of the Selling Writer*, "…The difference between the beginner and the pro is less one of talent or knowledge than of endurance."

I've seen writers come and go. I have friends who have dealt with personal life struggles and bumps in their careers. I've faced my share of hairpin curves myself, sometimes working through the struggle, other times needing time away. But success is always the result of perseverance. We own our achievements because we follow through and find ways to deal with the twists and turns.

In the beginning, even when I was tempted to quit, I'd ask myself, "What if the next book is the one? What if the next editor wants to buy the book?" And eventually a next book was the one. Ask yourself on a regular basis, "How badly do I want this?" and reevaluate your goals and the steps you're taking. Picture yourself where you want to be.

People always ask me for the secret to longevity; they want that one key to achieving success in this business, and the truth is, there is no one thing, no secret. But there are several things you can do to ensure you're on the right track and come closer to your goals.

- Believe in yourself.
- Find someone else who believes in you.
- Work hard.
- Push yourself.
- Look fear in the eye.
- Set quotas and deadlines.
- Get rid of distractions.
- Find inspiration.
- Polish. Edit, revise, and edit again.
- Study. Always be a student of your craft.
- Follow through, and complete every project.
- Surround yourself with positive people.
- Hold tight to the dream.
- Celebrate the steps along the way. Record your progress. Reward yourself often. Celebrate rejections because a rejection means you put yourself out there—and not everyone is brave enough or determined enough to do that.
- Find joy in the journey.

❝❞

One of the few things I know about writing is this: Spend it all, shoot it, play it, lose it, all, right away, every time. Do not hoard what seems good for a later place in the book, give it, give it all. Give it now ... Some more will arise for later, something better. These things fill from behind, from beneath, like well water.

Similarly, the impulse to keep to yourself what you have learned is not only shameful; it is destructive. Anything you do not give freely and abundantly becomes lost to you. You open your safe and find ashes.

—ANNIE DILLARD, AUTHOR OF *THE MAYTREES*

INDEX

WD WRITER'S DIGEST

Is Your Manuscript Ready?

Trust 2nd Draft Critique Service to prepare your writing to catch the eye of agents and editors. You can expect:

2ND DRAFT

- Expert evaluation from a hand-selected, professional critiquer
- Know-how on reaching your target audience
- Red flags for consistency, mechanics, and grammar
- Tips on revising your work to increase your odds of publication

Visit WritersDigestShop.com/2nd-draft for more information.

DEVELOP YOUR STORY ACROSS SEVERAL BOOKS

Writing the Fiction Series

KAREN S. WIESNER

From the Hunger Games Trilogy to the Jack Reacher series, from Harry Potter to Harry Dresden, there's no denying that writers—and readers—have caught series fever. But if you're contemplating writing a series, there are plenty of considerations you'll need to make first. *Writing the Fiction Series* is the complete guide to ensuring your series stays hot after the first, fourth, or even fifteenth book.

ble from WritersDigestShop.com and your favorite book retailers.
